DOUBLE 1

Ian Watson

Double Depression

SCHOOLING, UNEMPLOYMENT
AND FAMILY LIFE IN THE
EIGHTIES

GEORGE ALLEN & UNWIN
SYDNEY LONDON BOSTON

© Ian Watson 1985
This book is copyright under the Berne Convention. No
reproduction without permission. All rights reserved.

First published in 1985 by
George Allen & Unwin Australia Pty Ltd
8 Napier Street, North Sydney, NSW 2060 Australia

George Allen & Unwin (Publishers) Ltd
Park Lane, Hemel Hempstead, Herts HP2 4TE England

Allen & Unwin Inc.
Fifty Cross Street, Winchester, Mass 01890 USA

National Library of Australia
Cataloguing-in-Publication entry:

Watson, Ian.
  Double depression.

  Includes index.
  ISBN 0 86861 580 3.
  ISBN 0 86861 588 9 (pbk.).

  1. Family. 2. Interpersonal relations.
  3. Unemployed. 4. Youth—Employment.
  I. Title.

306.8'7

Library of Congress Catalog Card Number: 84−71571

Typeset by Setrite Typesetters, Hong Kong
Printed by Wing King Tong Co. Ltd, Hong Kong

Contents

Acknowledgements   vi

Introduction   1

Part I   Responses to Youth Unemployment
1   An investment in schooling   9
2   'Dole bread is bitter bread'   27
3   'The door's always open'   43

Part II   The Peer Group and the Family
4   The peer group as a battlefield   59
5   'The way it's always been'   79
6   Worlds apart   91

Part III   Class and Schooling
7   'We back answer like crazy'   111
8   'I wanted to get some discipline'   124
9   'Ghettoes for the wealthy'   136
10   Conclusion   147

Notes   155

Further reading   157

Index   159

Acknowledgements

A number of people have kindly read earlier versions of this book and have offered me valuable advice, critical comments and encouragement for which I am most grateful. I would particularly like to thank: Jill Bowling, Michael Gilding, Brian Martin, Beverley Pope, Therese Quinn, Simon Rosenberg, Basil Schur, Rachel Sharp and Bruce Smith.

During the research which provided the material used in this book, I benefited greatly from fruitful discussions with a number of interested people. I would particularly like to thank: Cherry Collins, Tim Hardy, Ann Hone, Beverley Pope, Therese Quinn, Simon Rosenberg and Bruce Smith.

I would also like to thank those schools I visited for their assistance in conducting the conversations. Similarly, I am grateful to the residents and staff of the youth refuge for their warm hospitality and their enthusiastic readiness to take part in the conversations.

Finally, I am greatly indebted to all those people who gave so freely of their time and their thoughts in the conversations I have recorded. I hope I have done justice to their words.

Introduction

A small black tape recorder is perched casually on a tuft of grass. Seated in a circle around it are four people, three of them young women in their last year of schooling, and myself, a researcher in social science. Beside us rises the bright, white concrete walls of their school. It is an austere, modern building, set in a new suburb where young married couples have moved to escape the mortgage squeeze.

I have come to talk with Karen, Sue and Laura about their experiences of schooling and their outlook on the future. The tape-recorder captures our conversation: the dribs and drabs of dialogue, the nervous pauses, the moments of prolonged reflection, the occasional outbursts of laughter and anger.

Karen, Sue and Laura are among 70 young people whom I sought out and talked with over the course of two years. At the time I was doing research for an academic degree. I eventually wrote a thesis based on these conversations but, like most academic theses, it was a thick book, densely written and barely readable to a non-specialist. However, because of my political commitment toward making useful knowledge widely accessible I could not rest content to see those many hours of conversation left buried on a university library shelf. This present book is the outcome of that commitment and in its style and layout it aims to offer to a wider audience those conversations and some of the insights they have given me.

With Karen, Sue and Laura, our conversation dwells for a long time on their experiences of school, in particular 'failure' at their school subjects. They quickly point out that they feel they are coping with their assignments, but their grades keep telling them they're failing. At the end of every term, their parents wait expectantly:

Sue: In class we work our guts out and all you get is an E. If you show your parents...you know a D or an E and you try to tell them that's not a fail, they say, 'Oh, you've failed', and everything. Pressures start coming on top of you, 'Oh, you'd better do better next time'.

Their self-esteem is also under threat. Repeated failures batter the ego. After a while, a kind of defeatism begins and a spiral of decline sets in:

Karen: I missed typing, you couldn't be bothered going...the marks are not going to change just because we don't go or anything...
You're gonna get an E anyway whether you try or not, so what's the difference.

The buffeting their self-esteem takes does not stay confined to the classroom. It forms part of a larger experience of coming to school in order to prepare for life:

Laura: You come here to work and study hard and everything and getting Es and Ds doesn't do anything for you. It gives you a poor outlook on what's ahead.

How do these young women explain what is happening to them? The assessment system is their main focus. But by 'assessment' they mean something quite different from what I understand. As an ex-teacher, I was disillusioned by an assessment system which I knew did not provide educational feedback, but served to officially certify those subjective experiences of failure and incompetence suffered by large numbers of struggling students. Assessment worked to legitimise the unequal parcelling out of life chances by convincing many young people that they had only minimal potential.

To these young women, 'assessment' is basically a matter of the unjust ways in which their subject grades are standardised. I pose a number of the questions which trouble many a teacher. Should graded assessment exist at all? Should teachers be the ones to confer it? Is it really possible to measure achievement on a literal or numerical scale? However, for these young women the immediate concern is the inequity of the arithmetic. What they resent above all is the unfairness of standardisation. This is a procedure whereby the school adjusts their raw scores according to a standard distribution curve. This meant that where, before standardisation, their scores would have earned them a B or a C grade; after passing through the computer, they give them only a D or an E. This drop in grade has occurred in nearly all their subjects, at the end of every term, for their last two years.

These women respond to this plight in an interesting way. They do not call for the overthrow of schooling: all of them desperately want to avoid the dole queues; all want the 'useful knowledge' which schools are meant to offer. Neither do they want to abolish assessment in its broad sense: they still want to take home grades, but ones which will please their parents. Instead, in a burst of flippancy, these young women suggest that the computer's plug be pulled out.

Why the computer? It is the shorthand expression for the standardisation procedures and it is the object of attack when these women feel their anger welling up. The computer has become a kind of go-between in the exchange between students and the school structure. Everyone, teachers, students, administrators, must live with the computer, particularly at enrolment times and at end of term. The computer is the readily available culprit. It serves as a convenient scapegoat, and at the same time, a mask hiding what stands behind it: the actual educational policies which endorse the unjust distribution of life's opportunities and rewards.

The computer is an explanation which excludes a whole domain of questions about how school fits into the economic system and into the social institutions which characterise contemporary society. Yet it is questions in these areas which would open a pathway to understanding these women's experiences.

In this book I intend to focus on how people explain their experiences of life. In particular I want to search for what symbols, like the computer, and what mental frameworks, present themselves to people as a means for understanding those experiences. These mental frameworks play a crucial part in shaping those experiences in particular ways, providing some people with the basis for taking greater control over their lives and robbing others of adequate means for resisting oppressive conditions.

It is seven months later and I am out shopping for groceries. I pass a small clothes shop and glancing in, see a face I recognise.

'Hello Karen. How are things?'

I stay talking twenty minutes, catching up on the last seven months of Karen's life. There was the graduation ball and the excitement of that final evening with her friends. Then followed weeks of relaxation, of swimming at the pool and window shopping in town. When she finally registered at the dole office she was surprised, and disappointed, to find the man behind the counter showed no interest in whether she was looking for work.

As the months dragged by, she found herself sinking into the familiar rut. She spent half the day in bed, soon got bored with window shopping, and seldom went out socially because she didn't have enough money.

Just last week this opening came: two days a week working in this clothes shop. She found the job through a friend of the family but she's not sure if she's going to be paid. The family connection makes it an embarrassing question and, what's more, they know she is on the dole.

'What about tech?' I ask. All three had told me earlier that they hoped to do secretarial courses at the local technical college and then get office jobs. Karen thinks Laura ended up going, but she's not sure about Sue. She's lost touch since school finished.

But what about herself? Why didn't she go? Karen answers vaguely, almost evasively. The course involved maths, science, English. She adds no more; this list is self-explanatory.

Then Karen begins to elaborate. School was enough. She wants no more to do with 'institutions' if she can avoid them. But she is still studying, she adds eagerly. She is doing a correspondence course in commercial art with one of those private correspondence schools. But it's not really working out very well. She pays $30 every month but receives no real help with her problems. The correspondence part is the trap. She writes and explains her problem, and they write back with the 'answer'. But somehow, it doesn't seem to help.

Karen refers to school again. She's glad to be free to work by herself, not to be trapped in an institution. Karen looks up defiantly, obviously proud of her independence. But then she pauses and, almost in a confessional manner, explains that she does not really seem to do much work without someone there to 'push her'. As I leave the shop, with a parting glance I dwell upon the irony: Karen has not failed at school; school has failed her, and countless others like her.

This episode, and the earlier conversation, are merely brief sketches in a larger canvas. The following pages will fill in the details of that picture. I offer excerpts from many of the conversations which I recorded during those two years. The names I have used are of course fictitious. Some of the people I talked with were in their final year of school, taking time out in their lunch break to talk to me about their experiences and their expectations. Some of the schools were ordinary state high schools, one was an alternative school and another was an elite private church school. Many of these people were heading for either tertiary study or the workforce.

There was another group I talked with, however, who had missed out on both these options. They were the unemployed young people whom I met in a youth refuge and in a low-cost accommodation barracks. With them the conversation often continued for several hours as a steady haze of smoke filled the air.

Some of the people I spoke with were the sons of wealthy business managers. Others were the sons and daughters of migrant labourers and factory workers. Their ages ranged from fourteen to eighteen and they divided equally into female and male.

In the chapters which follow I do not offer a comprehensive overview of these conversations. Rather, I have adopted a case study approach, where each chapter focuses on just one or two people. In this way it is possible to gain a much deeper appreciation of how people's ideas are intimately tied to their personal experiences and their social situations. The loss in terms of breadth is a small price to pay for these deeper insights. In many instances the people I focus on are typical, but sometimes they are unusual and not representative at all. This is not a weakness in my analysis because I am not making claims about what most people are like or what most people think. I am using the case study approach to explore the mental frameworks which lie behind people's thinking. It is these frameworks which are typical and which are widespread in contemporary society.

In particular, I focus on one of these frameworks, the ideology of individualism, and show how it lies behind the thinking of most of the young people with whom I spoke. This is an ideology which maintains that individuals are totally self-contained and owe nothing to their social or historical setting for the characteristics which they exhibit. The extension of this is that individuals hold their fate in their own hands and are responsible for whatever happens to them.

By contrast, I will argue throughout this book that it is crucial to avoid focusing on individuals as an end in themselves. Rather, to understand why people think and act in the ways they do, it is necessary to place them always within their social and historical context. This means examining the nature of social institutions (like the family), the underlying features of the economic system (such as work and the profit motive), and the basis for power relations (such as hierarchies). It will then emerge that people deal with all of these structures through various psychological strategies and that their ideas are the expression of these strategies.

Part I
Responses to Youth Unemployment

1
An investment in schooling

Sandy: I've got a friend and she dropped out of school at the end of fourth form. She was never any good at school, she never cared. 'I'm not going to go on to fifth form. It's a waste of time. It's stupid. I hate school.' Sorta thing. And at the moment she's on the dole and she just lies in bed all day. She sleeps in till midday, gets up, looks in the paper every now and then for a job, and once or twice I think she's bothered ringing up and applying for them. And you know, I thought, 'With that kind of attitude...'

She just says, 'I can't get a job, I can't find one anywhere.' But she's never looked.

Sandy glances up over the rims of her glasses. She has a serious expression on her face. Sandy is in her final year of school. The last six years have been a steady, often monotonous, march through all her studies. Sandy has set her sights on becoming a nurse and in a few short months she starts her basic training. Unlike her 'dropout' friend, Sandy stayed on at school and now she feels that the effort has been worthwhile. Like the other people in this chapter she has an investment in schooling: she has poured her energy into an extra two years of study in the hope that the dole queue can be avoided.

What kind of attitudes toward the unemployed does this kind of investment produce? This chapter will explore that question by focusing on the responses to youth unemployment by the people who have stayed on at school.

Sandy's comments are uncompromising. In Sandy's eyes her friend has only herself to blame for her fate. She dropped out of school because of the wrong 'attitude', and she's stuck on the dole because of that same attitude. In contrast, if Sandy were ever unemployed herself, she would show the kind of initiative she believes her friend so obviously lacks:

Sandy: If I was ever very unemployed I'd have enough knowledge to go and grab a few people and start up our own little business or something like that.

Sandy's outlook is based on the prevalent 'blame the victim' approach, attributing the reasons for unemployment to the characteristics of the people unemployed. This approach shuts out thinking about how social situations, like unemployment, are the result of structural changes in the economy. Such an approach is basically locked into considering symptoms, not underlying causes. Consequently, it nestles neatly into those conservative ideologies which proclaim that people have only themselves to blame for whatever happens to them. As Sandy says later, all the people who find themselves in boring factory jobs bring it upon themselves. It is their own fault for leaving school early:

Sandy: I think everyone have got the choice of whether they want to go on and get education or whatever, or whether they want to drop out there and then. Well, if they made that choice themselves, that they'd had enough of school and teachers, and they decided to drop out, well that's just stupid if they expect to go and get an exciting well-paid job. I mean you've got to take what you get and what you work for.

When Sandy is presented with an alternative point of view on unemployment, one which tries to present structural reasons, she finds little difficulty in sidestepping its arguments:

Sandy: Like there's a group of people. I don't know what they're called but they're always coming round to our school and to other schools complaining about unemployment and they put on all these plays. But you look at them and they're storming round and more or less blowing hell out of the government and out of the private enterprise and everything and saying, 'You should give us jobs', and kinda thing. And I just wonder how many of them have actually tried to go out and get a job. Whether they've just decided one day they get out of school, and they say, 'Oh, here I am and nobody's given me a job. I wonder what I should do? I know, I'll complain about it'.

Here Sandy puts words into the mouths of these people, words they would never say but which fit in with her way of presenting them. Sandy is able to avoid confronting their message by denigrating them as people. By dismissing this theatre troupe as no-hopers who are only capable of 'complaining', Sandy does not have to give any credence to what they are saying. This same approach is used to reject the message of feminism:

Sandy: Now if you get a whole lot of women complaining and saying, 'Oh we don't want to be stuck in the house all day. We want to take over men's jobs'. Sooner or later you're going to get a situation where they can't...can you imagine a lot of lady brickies racing around, and say if you're in a situation where they've gotta push a wheelbarrow full of cement up a very narrow plank, and they say, 'Oh God, I can't do it, it's too hard. The pressures on women today!' Now if the silly cows would get of out of the way and let the men take over that kind of thing, because it all gets back to the physical capabilities of the male.

Again Sandy puts words into people's mouths so as to present them in a certain way. She also chooses an extreme example, one which is barely relevant to the real issue. In essence, Sandy's perspective does not recognise the structural dimension of women's oppression. Instead it personalises the whole situation and turns it into a case of women who are 'complaining'.

There is a consistent thread in Sandy's thinking in all these passages. She continually focuses on individual people and not on social situations. Moreover, she thinks that these individuals are entirely responsible for their own fate and that if they find themselves in oppressive conditions it is their own fault, usually because they have the wrong 'attitude'.

Sandy's thinking is conditioned by the ideology of individualism, an ideology which treats individuals as entirely removed from their social context. This means that people's lives are explained solely in terms of their attributes, their strengths and weaknesses. These attributes in turn, are usually seen as 'naturally' belonging to the person and not as socially and historically produced.

The other people in this chapter, and indeed many throughout the book, also operate with this ideology. It is often not a conscious thing: individualism frequently works as a set of assumptions which lie behind people's thinking and structure it in certain ways.

The people below are all in their last years of secondary schooling. Many of them link schooling with unemployment. They focus on 'poor attitudes'—things like 'laziness', poor 'discipline', low 'initiative', and so on—as the key feature common to failure in both domains. This then allows schooling to be seen as one of the causes of unemployment. In the following conversations all the people speaking are basically blaming the attitudes of the unemployed for the existence of high youth unemployment and they either implicitly or openly aruge that they themselves do not possess these same attitudes.

The people staying on at school realise that many of the young unemployed are early school leavers. However, they see this as due to them possessing these poor attitudes and not as a commentary on the state of the labour market for 15- to 18-year-olds.[1]

The people still at school have stayed on, and in some cases, reluctantly returned, because they want to avoid the dole queues. Most of them therefore have this investment in schooling by which they need to believe that they will find work and that staying on at school has been worthwhile.

Pam and Michael draw on the examples of young people they know who have lacked the right attitudes, in this case the initiative and resiliency which makes for success:

> *Michael*: The unemployed school leavers just sit on the dole and do nothing.
> *Pam*: You know, 'It's hopeless, I can't find a job', so they just give up. And I was just recently looking through a paper and there was at least 50 jobs. A couple were without experience, and you know, they didn't even go for any.
> *IW*: You don't think the continual knockbacks that people get put them off it altogether, or do you think that shouldn't happen?
> *Michael*: Yes, I think it does, but you shouldn't let yourself get down.
> *Pam*: I went for a couple of casual jobs once. Tons of people went and I got knocked back and it didn't put me down and I eventually kept going and I got one.

As Michael sees it, it's all in one's own hands, it's nothing to do with the situation: 'you shouldn't let yourself get down.' As for Pam, she easily universalises her own experience: 'it didn't put me down and I eventually kept going and I got one.'

Again, emphasis on attitudes is at the heart of Michael's argument that the dole is a disincentive to work:

> *Michael*: They can get the same money on the dole or even more than working. You know, they look out and say, 'Why don't I just sit on my bum, I'm getting the same money for doing nothing'.
> *IW*: You think money's the main reason most people want a job?
> *Michael*: Well, it wouldn't worry me personally as long as I'm occupied, but you know, a lot of people, I'd say money has a lot to do with it. You know if you've got somebody sitting there giving you money for doing nothing and you've got to go out and work for the same thing, you know.

IW: You don't think you'd get bored in the long run, sitting there, taking it?
Pam: Oh, I would.
Michael: Oh I would personally myself, but I don't think a lot of people would. They'd rather sit back and do nothing.
Pam: People are lazy.

Both Pam and Michael have created a hypothetical 'other', an imaginary person against whom they contrast themselves. This 'other' has characteristics which they believe themselves not to have, for example, laziness and lack of initiative. In a similar way to Sandy, Michael even puts words into the mouth of this 'other': 'Why don't I just sit on my bum, I'm getting the same money for doing nothing.'

When people create a hypothetical 'other' like this it is a way of defining themselves more clearly. The self−other distinction is a common device for establishing self-identity. It's not unusual to hear phrases like 'Most people...but for me...' The disturbing thing about the way Michael and Pam use this distinction is that they present the 'other' in a stereotypical, almost dehumanised, way. A century ago, in Victorian times, many people in the ruling class believed that the working class did not feel things the same way that they did. Even today, many people in the West think that the poor in the Third World do not suffer because 'they're used to it'. Both these examples show that when the 'others' are presented in a dehumanised way, they are robbed of their capacity to feel, and thereby robbed of the justice they deserve from others.

The same thing is happening here with Pam and Michael. Michael thinks that most people wouldn't get bored doing nothing, but he would, that most people are motivated only by money, but he isn't. Pam thinks that most people are lazy, but she isn't.

In the western suburbs of a large city, where youth unemployment rates have regularly hovered around 40 per cent, a streak of optimism underlies the outlooks of Nick and Carol. Both believe that they will will find jobs:

IW: Both of you say you won't be unemployed, but in this area the unemployment rate is very high.
Nick: Yes, but the reason for that is people don't want to get a job, they just want to hang around or loaf all day. There's heaps of jobs around.

Carol: I reckon if they did a survey on the people who are unemployed, most of them are unemployed because they want to be unemployed.
Nick: They don't want to work.
Carol: They don't want to work but the people who want a job get a job.
Nick: Or, the people that are unemployed have had a job, didn't like it, so told the manager where to go.
Carol: Yeah, they're that kind of people. But like everyone I've known who's left who wanted a job and were serious about it, you know, not just joking, 'leaving, couldn't be bothered with school anymore', have got jobs. Like I know people who have been unemployed since fourth form for three or so years now but I know they're the kind of people that wouldn't be going knocking on people's doors, filling out every application they can, bothering to go to the commonwealth thing up the street.
Nick: They go down there once a fortnight to pick up their cheque.
Carol: They just don't try.

The main attitudes shown in this exposition are the lack of determination on the part of the unemployed and their generally poor outlook and work habits: 'they told the manager where to go' and 'they couldn't be bothered with school'. Even though Carol and Nick are probably thinking of particular people they know, they soon begin to generalise and create a hypothetical 'other': 'They're that kind of people.'

This self—other distinction plays an important psychological role for many of these young people. By defining themselves against a stereotypical 'other', they attempt to distance the prospect of unemployment by distancing the unemployed. This process involves assigning characteristics to the unemployed (such as laziness, lack of initiative, poor self-discipline, and so on) which contrast with the characteristics which they see themselves as possessing (or perhaps, hope they possess). If you draw the contrast between self and 'other' sharply enough, then it is much easier to believe that you'll never become the 'other'.

Nigel lives in the inner city. He is optimistic that at the end of the year when he leaves school he will find a job:

Nigel: But if you really want to, you know, you'll find a job anytime you want. Like I've tried before and found a job. It just takes a bit of your own time and you'll find it if you try hard enough.
IW: Do you think that applies to everyone?
Nigel: Yeah, that applies to most people.

IW: So all the people who are unemployed at the moment, they needn't be if they didn't want to be?
Nigel: Yeah, that's how it is. That's what I reckon because about two years ago I left school during fourth form and I wanted to do auto electrician then. And I went and tried all this area and I didn't find a job. Then I went to the industrial area and I found a job you know. There you can always find a job anywhere. It won't be hard, there's a lot of vacancies.
Matthew: I think I can get a job if I put my mind to it. No matter what it is at first, it's still money that comes in by you working and not someone supplying you...or you living off them. I think you can get a job if you really want one.
Nigel: Yeah, I've got a friend who left his work because they moved really far, the factory, and he just finished third or fourth form. He didn't have no experience or nothing and he was going to go on the dole but then decided against it. And he just went looking for work and he found a job straight away. I mean, about a week later. If he can find it, he's got...he doesn't have much experience and stuff like that, why can't we?

Nigel is optimistic because of previous experiences and the example of a friend. What is no doubt overlooked are all the counter-examples, all the friends who didn't find work. But then, both Nigel and Matthew have a strong psychological stake in seeing things this way. As Matthew puts it:

> No matter what it is at first, it's still money that comes in by you working and not someone supplying you...or you living off them.

Matthew is here voicing the almost universal aspiration of young people: the need for economic independence and self-respect. This aspiration gives the lie to the dole bludger myth, the perverse belief that young people would sooner get money for nothing than be financially independent and engaged in the adult world of work. Studies have shown that it is the social aspects of work rather than the economic rewards which young people value most in their jobs.[2] The pay packet counts, but that is mainly because it symbolises economic independence, being able to make one's own decisions about expenditure and lifestyle. For almost all young people, entry into the world of work is equated with achieving the identity and status of an adult.[3]

Why is the dole bludger myth so prevalent? After all, it has already been voiced by Pam and Michael and by Nick and Carol, and in the following pages it will arise often. Keith Windshuttle has shown how the dole bludger myth was systematically fabricated during 1974 and 1975 by politicians and the media as a way of dealing with problems produced by the vagaries of the labour market.[4] It was a cynical attempt to focus attention on the victims of unemployment in order to divert attention from the deepening recession and the failure of the government's policies to halt rising unemployment. Like most media myths, however, it relies on the existence of a fertile breeding ground within the community for it to take hold of people's minds. There are at least two reasons why the dole bludger myth was accepted widely in the community.

First, the deeply rooted nature of individualism means that people will invariably focus on individuals rather than structural factors when they are confronted with social problems. The media revels in this climate, a favourite device being the focus on personalities, on 'hardship cases' or on deviants. The media rarely deals with the wider social and historical context in which events arise.

Second, the nature of work under capitalism is such that human labour is only deemed worthwhile when it is spent on producing goods and services which are profitable. Pouring one's energy into activities which are socially worthwhile, but unprofitable in the marketplace, does not count as real 'work'. As is well known, this is the case with most housewives and of those people who do voluntary community work. They are not recognised as officially unemployed (so as to keep the figures down) but neither are they paid a wage or recognised as being fully employed.

The outcome of these two things, the focus on individuals and what counts as work in a capitalist society, is that unemployed people are invariably denigrated as not really 'working', no matter how fruitfully they spend their time.

Paul is a good example of this attitude towards work. The importance of being in paid employment takes on strong moral overtones in his attack on 'dole bludgers':

IW: As far as the dole goes then, you're saying you just don't like the idea of handouts. You don't mind other people getting the dole?
Paul: Well, if they can live with their consciences, that's alright with me.
IW: You still think there's something wrong with it?
Paul: I couldn't live with my...I could not live with my conscience.

I just couldn't.
IW: But if you had no money, you had no job?
Paul: I wouldn't go on the dole, still wouldn't. I'd starve to death instead of going on the dole. I would, I really would. I know $58 a week for nothing sounds really good but I'd rather work my guts out.

I know I can get a job. I know I can always get a job even if it's for $30 a week on the farm. I mean anyone can get a job if they really want one, that's my view. But a lot of people say 'Bullshit'. I think nowdays people are a bit more choosy and I don't think people are willing to get their back into it and work for $30 a week because they say, 'Look I want more than that. I want this, that and the other', and putting up all these conditions and saying, 'I'd like a job I'd enjoy and I'd like this, that and the other'.

And they're not willing to go to work and get $30 a week and if they're desperate, instead of going on the dole, I think it'd do a lot of people a lot better if they did actually work for a minimum, not very much money at all.

Again, the whole situation of unemployment is pictured in terms of attitudes; all its complexity is reduced to a person's state of mind. This perspective totally ignores the ratio of jobs to vacancies in the labour market. Throughout the present recession there has generally been only one job vacancy for every twenty unemployed people. Moreover, unemployment is always heavily regionalised. Some cities and suburbs may offer good job prospects; others—like Wollongong, for example—are extremely bleak. It is absurd to argue that anyone can get a job if they really want one. Yet Paul thinks this way. Why?

Basically, there is a tendency to universalise one's own experiences and ignore the distinctive features of other people's situations. Paul has always found work when he has needed it, and he attributes this to having the 'right attitude'. In fact, Paul worked on a farm during the holidays for $30 a week. As he sees it, if he can do that, why can't everyone else?

All the people so far have focused almost exclusively on attitudes. There were some people who introduced situational factors into their discussion about unemployment, but explanation by recourse to attitudes was never far away.

Lucy, a 16-year-old whose boyfriend is unemployed, focuses on background factors, particularly the operation of peer group influences:

IW: If you think these openings are there then, why are there still so

many young people unemployed in this area?
Lucy: I suppose because they don't want jobs. They just don't want to work.
IW: What do you think has caused unemployment?
Lucy: People that are slack that drop out of school because they hate school, they don't like to learn. And I suppose when they drop out their mates want to be like them because they want to be able to have free time and get money at the same time. And that's when the guys get in trouble too, you know. They start stealing because they don't get enough on the dole and then they're in trouble with the police and it just keeps going on in a vicious circle.

Though Lucy offers an added dimension to the familiar 'school dropouts' explanation, this exposition is still rooted in the idea of attitudes. For Lucy the real cause of unemployment is still people's attitudes: their slackness and their hating school. All that this added dimension shows is that the peer group worsens an already existing disposition.

It is usual to find that the diagnosis of any problem determines the solution offered. Lucy is no exception, and she suggests that the answer to unemployment is for the unemployed to show some initiative: for the young men to make furniture in their backyards and for the young women to bake cakes.

Some of the people still at school showed some sympathy towards the unemployed and refrained from engaging in the kinds of blanket condemnations illustrated above. This group alludes to 'dole bludgers', but qualifies this by referring to examples to people trying hard to find work but not succeeding.

Don is typical of this group. He is in his final year of school, and after an unsettled period in the early and middle years of high school, has 'settled down'. He works hard and now sees his ambition to join the police force near at hand. For Don, the image of the 'dole bludger' comes vividly to mind:

> You see kids wandering around town, all going to the dole office and they're only sixteen and that and they're picking up cheques. And they've probably been doing it for two or three years. Oh. If they were sixteen they've probably only just started, you know, for the length of time that they're going to do it they'll probably be nineteen before they wake up and say, 'God, I'm married. What am I going to do?'

Don then proceeds to qualify this image with another: the example of his own father's period of unemployment:

IW: If you can't find work will you go on the dole?
Don: Yes. I would.
IW: What about those people who say that going on the dole is a disincentive, and it's a bit of a stigma and things like that?
Don: They've probably never been out of work. They've probably had a job all their life.

My father was off work for a time and he'd worked for the whole of his life, ever since he was fourteen and suddenly he had to get unemployment benefits to support his family. And I went in with him and I saw him sit there and it took him a good half an hour just to get in the line and then he just walked out. You know. And he was just so put down with himself that he couldn't get a job and he had to go on unemployment benefits... He found it hard to adjust but after a while he accepted it. You know, because there was no other way he could have supported his family and that was his priority so...
IW: It was just the first time that he walked away from the line?
Don: Yeah. When he come back and filled it all in, what made it sort of acceptable to him, it was sickness benefits, not unemployment benefits. He was actually entitled to sickness benefits and when they told him that it sorta cheered him up. But the stigma for him was so great that he couldn't even sorta face standing in the line because all the other guys there sorta had long hair and thongs and he just thought: 'What the hell am I doing in a line with these people? I've worked for the whole of my life.' You know, it was his last resort. It wasn't something he took lightly.

Don clearly perceives that the work ethic is crucial to a person's self-esteem and he is thus sympathetic to the psychological damage induced by unemployment. Nevertheless, the dole bludger myth is not entirely dismissed, merely qualified. It hovers around a second image: that of the long-haired, thong-wearing crowd against whom his father is continually contrasted. Their appearance is, for Don, a sure sign of their poor attitude and contrasts sharply with his father, properly dressed and primed with a strong work ethic.

Don has thus refrained from a blanket condemnation of the unemployed, but he has done this by dividing them into two: the 'worthies' and the 'unworthies'. And the distinction is one grounded in individualism. These two groups differ mainly in terms of attitudes, though it is the physical appearance which provides the litmus test for these.

Not only is his father contrasted with the 'bludgers' in the dole queue, but Don contrasts himself with them as well. In the earlier passage above he criticised them for not having 'woken up' to themselves. In the following passage, where Don talks of his future plans, he is proud of having 'woken up' to himself:

> *Don*: While I'm single I can sorta survive on a lower wage. But by the time I get married I've got to have so much in the bank for a house, a car, you know. I've got to be earning so much to pay for a wife, a kid. You know, it sort of influences you. You gotta sorta think, 'Well if I work now and I'm married in five years, how much money will I have in the bank?' And it plays a big part in what you set your goals at.
>
> . . .
>
> A lot of people have left school and they don't seem to have any plans for the future. They just sort of get a job now and you know, 'Give mum twenty bucks board. I've got fifty bucks left for the weekend'. And they can afford sort of to buy a small car and go down the coast and do what they like.
>
> But as soon as they get married and they're only earning just over a hundred bucks a week in their pocket, that's not a lot of money to pay for a house and a wife and food and the car. And I think it's a really big blow to drop from really enjoying yourself to sorta really having to watch what you spend and they just haven't planned for it, I don't think.
>
> *IW*: What should they do?
>
> *Don*: Oh, I think it all starts here. I used to sort of bum around at high school. Sorta enjoy myself. 'Ah school's nothing important.' I got to me last two years and I woke up and said, 'Well this is it. In two years you're gonna come out of here with a bit of paper that's gonna get you a job for the rest of your life'.
>
> And I thought, 'Well, if I come out with mediocre grades like I did in early high school, I'll get a mediocre job. If I come out with high grades I've got the chance of getting a high job'. And I think it really influenced me to think, 'Well in five years, you know, inflation might be such and such, you know'. I just didn't sorta ignore what was happening.

Don paints a particular image in this self-characterisation: he is aware of reality, he is prudent in his planning, his general outlook is a 'responsible' one. All these features stand out for him in sharp contrast to the characteristics of the long-haired, thong-wearing crowd, the no-hopers of the dole queue. They are the people he would have been if he hadn't woken up to himself and become the responsible person he now sees himself to be.

Marg is a 15-year-old who is still at school but has left home and is at present living in a youth refuge. Several of the other young people in the refuge are unemployed and are sitting around while Marg is talking. Marg's initial response to the issue of unemployment avoids references to the unemployed altogether. She focuses instead on government responsibility and the role of migrants. After she is provoked by a question which 'blames' the unemployed, she proceeds to defend them, referring to her conscientious brothers as examples. However, this immediately confronts her with another domain of personal experience, that of the young people living in the youth refuge:

IW: Why is unemployment so high?
Marg: Fraser. [Laughs] Oh partly him, you might as well not say Fraser but the whole government.
IW: In what way?
Marg: Well look at what they're doing to the country. They're just completely wrecking it...I don't know. I don't know much about politics but I'd say they did have a fair bit to do with it. And also because of, like you go into a shop and Australians don't own any of the shops here I'd say. I'd say most Italians, Greeks and so on own them. And it's true, it's really true.
IW: You don't think it's anything to do with the people that are going for jobs, that they don't want to work, cause that's what a lot of people reckon?
Marg: Well, I saw my brothers when they were out of work and they really tried hard. They'd get up at six o'clock of a morning, get the morning paper and look really hard for jobs. But you see the kids here at the refuge and they couldn't give two shits. Excuse my language but I mean that Col, it's true. Compared to some people that you see...
Col: I can't get a job.
Marg: Yeah, but you don't try hard enough. You see some people and they are really struggling hard to get a job and yet you see other people...
Col: Hang on. What's the point in getting a job if I'm going to Darwin.
Marg: To get the job to get money. You need money to go to Darwin.
Col: Yeah, well I look in the paper.
Marg: What. About eleven o'clock, twelve o'clock?
Col: No.
Marg: You do so. Don't bullshit.
Col: I looked at it as soon as I got up this morning.
Marg: Yeah and everyone has to pull you out of bed.
Col: Who pulled me out of bed yesterday morning?

> *Marg*: Yesterday morning? Yeah well you don't try hard enough, that's just it. If you want to get somewhere you have to try and what year did you drop out of school?
> *Col*: Second form.
> *Marg*: Yeah. See if you didn't drop out of school you'd still be there now.
> *Col*: No I wouldn't.
> *Marg*: Well you might have a job by now, if you didn't drop out.

This passage offers a fascinating glimpse into how two people argue, of how different avenues open and close as the attack advances and recedes. It shows how much a person's self-esteem is under threat when they cannot argue convincingly. But what this excerpt also shows is that individualism is paramount. Again the unemployed are divided into 'worthies' and 'unworthies' and the links with school failure are highlighted. Again the destiny of the individual is seen to rest exclusively in their own hands.

Carl is sixteen and living in the same youth refuge. He is at present unemployed and is one of the people Marg has in mind in her condemnation of the 'unworthies'. In the following brief biography, Carl rejects any attempt to explain things in situational terms, because he interprets such arguments as blame upon his parents:

> *Carl*: From the beginning of first form I was in and out of institutions and stuff. I've been in nearly every institution there is to go to.
> *IW*: Why do you reckon that was? What was happening to you? Whose fault was it do you reckon?
> *Carl*: Oh, mine of course.
> *IW*: Why?
> *Col*: It wasn't nailed down, so he took it.
> *Carl*: When you go up and, this is just an instance, when you go up and rob a bank, you know, you can't say, 'The bank teller made me do it'. It was your own fault, your own...
> *IW*: Some people would say it was the way you were brought up or the situation you found yourself in?
> *Carl*: It wasn't the way I was brought up. I've got very high respect for my parents now.

Carl is moving here in the world of individualism where the social situation is irrelevant. Consequently, when it is not possible to blame his parents or the bank teller, that leaves only one explanation: he is to blame. However, later in the conversation, Carl is voicing resentment at his harsh treatment by the courts and now has a different purpose. He now wants to argue for the inclusion of situational factors, because he regards them as extenuating circumstances. He now has a strong interest in shifting the blame away from himself:

> *Carl*: I think the courts should take more consideration in cases. They should look at the background properly. Instead most courts just say: 'One break and enter, steal. Right, criminal offence. Bang.' But maybe there's something behind it that could have caused it, you know, family, background, friends. Things, instances like that.

Carl is now in a different world, the world of the social worker where environmental factors are used to explain individual 'pathologies'. The general framework is still individualistic (because the individual is still the focus of attention, still the 'case') but now the social situation is at least recognised. Carl's movement from one world to another shows that his judgments are not constrained simply by ignorance. It is also a question of strategies: sometimes people use conversations to explore their feelings, sometimes to extend their thinking, sometimes simply to preserve their self-esteem, and so on.

These strategies can change in the course of a single conversation. At a later stage in our conversation, Carl returned to his earlier perspective. There were no immediately threatening consequences this time, so he speculated freely. Once more he was back in the world of individualism:

> Society is what you make it really. Either you can be a bum and sleep under a park bench or you can get a job and work or you can go on the dole and share a house with somebody. Society is what you make it.

It seems ironic that the person making these comments is, himself, so far removed from their application. Carl, Col and the other unemployed youths staying in the refuge are further from achieving this ideal than almost any other group in society. Their poverty, their homelessness, their low formal education and poor job skills, their generally low self-esteem, all these factors mean that these young unemployed people are less in control of their lives than most people. Yet here they are strongly voicing this myth of the self-determining individual. It is a myth which describes how things ought to be, not how they are, and this possibly explains why it has such a powerful appeal for them.

Finally, there is Barbara, a person who vigorously rejected the dole bludger myth and referred instead to capitalism. She was attending an alternative school where criticisms of both capitalism and patriarchy were common currency. These criticisms, moreover, were based largely on the counter-cultural values of the sixties. Most of her friends outside school were unemployed and pursued the lifestyle encapsulated in these counter-cultural values. Not surprisingly, Barbara does not refer to the characteristics of the unemployed at all in her explanation:

> *Barbara*: I'm not really sure what makes unemployment but it's just an easy thing to say, it's the economy. I suppose it's the reason why people vote for Hayden or Fraser. But they're foolish, none of them can change it. They haven't got power over it.
> *IW*: What is necessary to do anything about it? Who can change it all?
> *Barbara*: Get rid of capitalism I suppose. I mean America controls Australia and so if America did something I suppose it would affect us. I think probably it all relates back to human nature or something, it's so hard to define. If we got rid of greedy people there might be more employment.
>
> . . .
>
> I look at it from a completely illogical point of view I suppose. I see it as mean and nasty humans and, you know, capitalism and...
> *IW*: What's the answer to unemployment?
> *Barbara*: Well I think the answer is an individual one. I mean for me I see the answer as something a bit like Nimbin is supposed to be. Which is like sort of try and forget money a bit and work for your own, you know, what you want and not be greedy. You know, not say, 'Well I want to have a 25-inch colour television set'. So you're just working for your own food and clothing.
>
> . . .
>
> But you see some people are too far removed from that so it's not the solution for everybody. It's the solution for me and perhaps other people like me.

In her comments Barbara partly recognises that explanations are to be found by looking at the overall situation, capitalism in this case. She is also aware that there are alternative social arrangements which produce different situations, for example, Nimbin.

Despite this awareness, Barbara's outlook is still conditioned by the ideology of individualism. Her solution to a situational problem is an individual one and she admits this solution would only work for some people.

Even when Barbara does refer to the overall situation, capitalism, she soon reduces it to individuals. Capitalism quickly becomes merely a descriptive label for the greedy behaviour of people and this in turn is due to 'human nature or something'. Barbara's greedy people with their television sets is simply an updated version of the classic position of bourgeois political theorists in the eighteenth and nineteenth century. Instead of seeing people's characteristics, their greed or generosity, their hatred or compassion, as the product of their circumstances and the kind of society they lived in, these political theorists converted these social characteristics into natural ones. They then proceeded to explain the kind of society by the 'human nature' of the people living in it. By inverting reality in this way, these apologists of the ruling class sought to entrench the existing inequalities in economic and political power within a framework that appeared 'natural' and thus not open to the prospect of change.

The legacy of these political theorists is still around today. Notions of human nature, in which social and historical features of human development are naturalised, and thereby made eternal, abound in the area called 'commonsense'. Every day, one hears expressions like, 'it's only natural that...', 'that's human nature', and so on. The political consequences of this, particularly the stifling of the potential for change, are also part of that legacy.

Returning to Barbara, it is clear that her comments reflect incomplete knowledge about the nature of capitalism. What this means is that as people proceed in their explorations into areas of greater ignorance, areas where they begin to speculate more, so ideas drawn from their commonsense move to fill the breaches in their knowledge. 'Commonsense' is thus the crevice through which individualism is smuggled into Barbara's explanation and keeps her tied to a perspective which is at variance with her own political sympathies.

Throughout this chapter it has become clear that individualism underlies the thinking of nearly all these young people. The psychological strategies which are tied into this perspective induce young people still at school to adopt unsympathetic positions towards their unemployed peers. Basically the people still at school explain youth unemployment by rubbishing the young unemployed and thus attempt to distance the prospect of their own unemployment. This serves to justify staying on at school and steels these people against the fear of the future.

But the price paid for this reassurance is a heavy one. Because the focus is on individuals, these people are denied the opportunity to gain a better understanding of their society, particularly its structural features. For one thing, they have been denied any real understanding of the economic causes of unemployment.

By ruling out compassion for those currently unemployed, individualism also weakens the prospect of avoiding self-blame if these young people find themselves unemployed after they have left school. As the next two chapters will show, the severity of the 'dole blues' can often depend on keeping self-esteem intact and avoiding destructive patterns of self-absorption.

2
'Dole bread is bitter bread'

> On an island in a river
> How that bitter river ran
> I grew on scraps of charity
> In the best way that you can
> On an island in a river
> Where I grew to be a man
>
> And the hunger of the many
> Filled the bellies of the few
>
> For dole bread is bitter bread
> Bitter bread and sour
> There's grief in the taste of it
> There's weevils in the flour
>   Dorothy Hewett

By February 1978 the total number of unemployed people in Australia finally passed the number unemployed during the Great Depression of the 1930s. The historical parallels between the 1930s and the 1980s are many. The unemployed have again been blamed for the failure of the capitalist economy to provide work and the unemployed are again suffering the material deprivation and the psychological decline which their grandparents knew.

Particularly hard hit are the long-term unemployed. Studies carried out in Europe during the 1930s[5] found that the long-term unemployed suffered a range of psychological symptoms as a result of their physical hardship and their emotional distress. They suffered personality changes such as the onset of chronic depression, increased irritability and a severe loss in self-esteem. Their outlook was characterised by a general sense of powerlessness which often lapsed into fatalism.

The world of work gives to people a sense purpose, a basis for organising their time around a set of activities. When denied work, people cannot always replace that pivot in their lives. Research done in a small Austrian village in the 1930s where the whole community was unemployed, concluded that startling changes had occurred in people's sense of time. Not only did the community as a whole reorient its rhythm around the payment of benefits (replacing Sunday as the central day of the week) but for the unemployed individual, the enforced idleness led to an aimless and empty existence. With the onset of unlimited free time, people found they lost the ability to manage their time fruitfully.[6]

I spent some time among some long-term unemployed youths and I found that this picture of the 1930s was emerging again. However, where in the 1930s many unemployed youths set off for the countryside to find seasonal work, today the direction of travel is in the opposite direction. Like a magnet the cities lure the unemployed youth, drawing them into a twilight world of poverty, drug addiction and petty theft.

Bill, Andy and Bob are three such long-term unemployed youths. My conversation with them takes place in a low-cost accommodation barracks. In the adjacent wings of the building live other homeless people, mostly old men who are alcoholics. It is not always an easy coexistence:

> *Andy*: We don't go around pissing and shitting in hallways like the old alcoholics do. You wanna come down and look in my block. I'll show you this big stain. Half of it's still there and you can walk up and you can see the fucking big mark and you can smell it and you go for a walk up there and I bet you wouldn't even live in it. And we have to.

The room is almost bare, relieved only by bright posters on the walls and a small stereo pounding out heavy rock music. The three youths are sitting on the bed, passing around a can of beer. On a shelf on the wall opposite is a small row of tinned food, neatly arranged and very conspicuous. On another shelf, to the side of the bed, is a small glass jar containing marijuana seeds. They fidget with the jar from time to time. Bill, who left school at fourteen, has been unemployed now for four years. Andy has spent several years unemployed, though this has been interspersed with occasional temporary labouring jobs. Bob has worked as a show labourer for a number of years but is now unemployed and heavily in debt. His previous job is a liability when he now looks for work:

Bob: I had the same problem when I was on the show. Like showies got a bad name as you know, and when I first came back to town, getting a job, 'Oh what've you been doing?'
'Working the side shows for the last two years.'
'Oh yeah, we'll ring you.'
You don't hear nothing.

My conversation with these young people revolves almost exclusively around the theme of unemployment: of the poverty it produces, the stigma associated with it, and the differences between being employed and unemployed. All three blame their schooling, to some extent, for their unemployment:

Bill: I think this Education Departments' got it wrong, it's got the wrong idea of teaching. If they got their heads screwed on right... If they started teaching what you need to know, then I don't reckon you'd have this unemployment quite as bad.

The others elaborate on this by pointing out that insufficient attention was paid to their learning problems and that the curriculum was not vocationally oriented. As Bill put it, somewhat sarcastically:

I can't handle getting taught something I don't need to know, Like I reckon that's just a waste of time. Like you go to school, you're in a history class and you're getting taught about what colour socks the German soldiers wore or something. You know, these really trivial things that you don't really need to know. It won't help you at all.

Bob resented the hypocrisy of his school:

A few years ago when I was at school, they never taught you nothing. In metalwork class you just make tiny little things. You weren't allowed to touch some machines.
   Like they say, when you join the school, 'We'll call you Ladies and Gentlemen because we treat you like adults here.' But then after a couple of months, you just get treated like shit.

It was apparent in the last chapter that this idea of a link between schooling and unemployment is common among most of the young people still at school. They, however, laid the responsibility not on the teaching or the curriculum, but squarely on the attitudes of the students. Those people looked around themselves and picked out the potential unemployed on the basis of attitudes: those who didn't work hard, those who showed no self-discipline, and so on. Bill's father also shares this view that school performance brings its 'just rewards':

Bill: My old man just doesn't want to know me cause I'm unemployed. He said when I get a job I'll speak to you... Me father just looks at it, 'Oh well, because you didn't go well at school you deserves what you get and that's how it is'.

In one sense, Bill and his friends agree with these other assessments. Andy, for example, admits that when at school he was totally unprepared to accept authority and rebelled against the authoritarian context of his schooling by withdrawing from learning. The legacy of this experience, and its implications for any future educational prospects, are apparent in the following:

Andy: The CYSS[7] drop-in-centre is like school to me and I won't have anything to do with any kind of schooling. Someone sitting in front of me telling me what to do. I just can't do it and a job is so hard. I've kept jobs, the longest job I've kept is six months. Yeah. I just can't handle discipline.

Once on the dole the whole question of schooling becomes irrelevant to Bill and his friends. Their main concerns become questions of day-to-day survival. The difficulties of finding and holding work are heavily compounded by the persistence of the dole bludger myth, which hovers like a dark shadow:

Andy: I get labouring jobs now and then. I'm doing me fucking best they just say, 'Dole bludger', and once you're a dole bludger that's it, you're done. You cash a cheque they think instantly whether you've had work or not, they still think you're a dole bludger...

Even within the family, Andy meets the same reception:

Andy: My brother if I ask him for a cigarette or a dollar, he'll just go Smack! He thinks I'm a fucking dole-bludging cunt. That's what he calls me.
IW: That's your brother?
Andy: My brother.

As the months pass there is a continual struggle against the poverty that comes from trying to live on $36 a week:

Bill: Like the dole's a real rage for the first couple of months and then after that it's a different story totally.
Bob: Yeah, you get into debt too much.
Bill: Oh, everything just goes wrong. I reckon there's heaps of suicides cause of it... I've known someone who's just slashed his wrists to pieces just cause he couldn't get a job and he just had no

money and he was just so badly in debt and just the whole world was just caving in on him.

If a cheque ever fails to arrive, it can mean near disaster. Andy had this happen recently:

Andy: I'm starving as it is. I really starve... We go to his girlfriend's whose mum works at a restaurant and she serves food. So that's something to eat. So that's pretty good. Oh Bill's got a couple of tins of food up there, which we eat out of. See up there on the shelf.
Bill: Red Cross.
Andy: We go to Red Cross, Saint Vinnies. You just really can't survive on the dole...
Bill: Last time I bought new clothes was three years ago.
Andy: I stole these... That's how you do things these days.
Bill: You don't buy anything on the dole. You just can't.

There is also the general psychological decline which sets in from months of being continually rejected:

Bob: ...there's a lot of us don't like working, like sometimes I just feel like, 'Oh, I don't want to do anything today'. For a week I'll just feel like sitting around doing bugger all and the next week you feel like getting out and doing something. But a lot of people are just in downers all the time.
Bill: You find a lot of unemployed people that just don't care anymore because they've been put down so much they're just like that. If say you applied for about ten jobs a week, you know that's a lot of jobs you know and you didn't get anything for a whole year, you'd be so fed up with it you'd just get lazy and that's the end of it. You just give up. Some people, you know a lot of people, just give up totally, you know a hundred per cent there's no way they want to have a job, they're so fed up with it.

This pattern of decline follows a cyclical pattern:

IW: Have you given up all hope of ever getting a job or how do you feel about it?
Bill: Well I have sort of given up hope sorta. How would you say it? Yeah, at times you're sorta...it's just like a big cycle. It happens every so many months. You get to a stage, 'Oh yeah I'm gonna get a job'. You're so determined, you go out. Just nothing happens. Then you're in a real downer situation for about a month or so and then you go up. It's just a big cycle. You just go through it all the time.

Despite this emphasis on their personal decline, there is still an acute recognition that the situation of unemployment is responsible for these outcomes:

> *Bill*:   The problem with being on the dole, I reckon if you've been on it too long and someone hits you with a job, you sort of freak out, you don't know what to do, whether to take it or not cause you sorta think: Look if you're on the dole too long you just get used to it and its just a way of life and a job is such a big step when you've been on the dole for a few years. You get so immune to it, you know, it's really bad...
>
> I've found at times I've just been so unenergetic, even to hand me dole form in, like you've only got to do that every second week. I just get to the stage where I just hand it in late all the time. You just get so unmotivated. You just get fed up with it all.

The daily routine which accompanies dole living reinforces this pattern of losing a sense of time:

> *IW*:   How do you fill in a day?
> *Bill*:   If I'm out determined to get a job I get up early, go out, look at CES[8] boards, papers, apply for whatever I can and then if I haven't got to go for an interview I come home and just do whatever. But if you're not looking for a job you get up at twelve o'clock, walk around, just sit, listening to music, go and see somebody. And drugs have got a lot to do with it then.
> *Bob*:   You got nothing to do, so you think 'Oh well...'
> *Bill*:   When you got nothing to do, that's when crime, drugs, everything just comes into it.
> *IW*:   How do you pay for the drugs, cause the dole's not even enough to live on?
> *Bill*:   Yeah, well...
> [General laughter]
> *Bill*:   Oh well, it's a big rip-off really. Like you just sort of listen around. Like when you're on the dole you've got heaps of time for finding out where's the best to buy, and all that. And you sort of buy what you can with your cheque. Like I've spent $100 just on drugs with me cheque, bought that, come back here and sort of divided in it into smaller lots, and sold it. You can sorta make money out of it that way. But not a great deal, you'd probably make about $20 or $30 and have some for yourself to smoke. If you go into anything heavy, like smack, that's a different story, you got to get out and work for it then. Illegally work for it that is.
>
> *IW*:   Do you ever think about the future?
> *Bob*:   I'm only really thinking about what's going to come up tomorrow.

Bill: When you're on the dole you just think about what you're going to do tomorrow. You don't look at it as in about four or five months ahead or anything like that. The furthest you'd think ahead would be about two weeks. At the moment I'm just living day by day...

The psychological defences that emerge to counter the poverty and aimlessness of dole living revolve heavily around drugs. But this is not without its drawbacks. At one stage in our conversation, Bill loses track of what he is saying. He comments:

Bill: I've got what you call bad short-term memory. That's from smoking drugs a lot. I just sorta forgot what we were talking about then.
Bob: Yeah, it stuffs you up. I'm the same. Since I've been back in town I've been smoking every day. Stoned nearly all day and all night.
Andy: I've been in a daze for about four months.
Bob: The only time when I'm straight is when I go to me girlfriend's.
Bill: If you're into smoking drugs, and someone walks up to you and gives you a job and you start, that is very very hard. Very hard. You need about two weeks just to straighten out, to get your head together and say, 'Right. Got a job. Do it'.
IW: Can you give it away whenever you want?
Bill: Dope's not addictive, that's why I'm smoking it.
Bob: It's addictive in a way.
Andy: There's a lot of people who can't quit from smoking dope you know.
Bill: It's not a physical thing, it's a mental thing. You just got to be stoned cause you can't handle being straight because the world's so fucked or whatever reason you've got. You've just got to be stoned all the time to feel better.
Bob: I was travelling back from the coast, I was straight all the way. I got home I was shaking so bad. I had a bong, after one bong, I was sweet, no worries.

The other defence to the continual battering which their self-esteem takes is to give up the fruitless job search:

Andy: I've given up looking for a job. If a job comes to me or I find out about a job I'll go to it but I won't look for a job.
IW: Why?
Andy: Just no way. Cause I've just had so many disappointments, just get fucking so fed up.

But these defences do not go unchallenged. Both drug taking

and giving up the job search come in for massive criticism in the outside community:

Andy: We've got nothing. We can sit around here and smoke drugs all day. We get put down for that, cause we're druggos. We drink, we're alkies. We fucking walk around the streets, you get called a dole bludger cause you're just walking the streets. You get put down for that. And places like Pot Black where you got pool tables and pinnies but they close places like that down cause criminals meet there.

Places like the CYSS drop-in centres partly fill this need for diversion. We saw earlier that Andy is turned off by his memories of school. Bill and Bob have a different view:

Bob: The only purpose to that [CYSS] is to keep you off the streets. I think it's just to keep you amused while you're on the dole, just to keep you from crime and that.
Bill: It's a good idea. It builds your motivation up. Like if you go in there and get with some people, 'Righto, we're doing this pottery, you want to come in on it?' You're sorta getting into it. You're sorta doing things then and then you sorta start getting motivated. Then you start looking for jobs again. For people who have just given up and they go to places like that, it gets them back up to the stage where they can go and look for a job again.
IW: Is that a good thing?
Bill: Yeah.
IW: But then they just get knockbacks again.
Bill: Yeah, but places like that, just keeps your hopes alive, gets you motivated really. Cause you can get to a stage when you just sit in a house, listen to records all day and all night and go to sleep and that's all you're doing. Like I've sat in a house for about a week, and just never got out, just to the shops to buy food and then just come back.
Andy: The only good thing thing about that is you get time to think. You do a lot of thinking and you just think, 'Fuck, what've I done?'
IW: What kinds of things do you think about?
Andy: That's right, there's nothing you can think about. What I keep thinking is how stoned I got and how many good women I rooted. That's about all. I can't think of anything sorta like, 'Gees it was good at work today'. You just got nothing to think about cause you're always sitting around.
Bill: When you're on the dole you can work out how many bad people there are in this world. Like all these people who are earning heaps and heaps of money, they're criminals sorta to unemployed people...
Andy: They're doing fuck all.
Bill: ...and to them, we're the same. It's two different sorts of people really.

At one stage Bill refers to employed people as 'the working class' and strongly distinguishes them from people like himself. Paid employment, no matter how stultifying or how socially useless, is nevertheless the key definer of social prestige in a capitalist society. Windshuttle has written:

> Work defines our standing with our fellows, our self-esteem, our income level, the scope of our lives. It is the most basic definition of our concept of humanity.[9]

Bill and his friends feel the force of this every day on the streets:

> *Bill*: Some really well-off people they give you that look, you know, you're a degenerate, you know.
> *Bob*: Sometimes you'll be walking along the street, just walking along like you can only have old clothes on and that, except your work clothes, and they sorta walk past and they seem, it's like they're about a hundred foot tall, and they're just looking down on a piece of dog shit, that's how they're looking at you like that.

When they encounter the put downs among their own mates the bite of being workless is felt even sharper:

> *Andy*: I've had mates working, they go, 'Oh we're paying tax for you'. How they think it is, the money out of their pockets coming into us.

This ostracism knows no national boundaries. Here are the comments of another unemployed youth, 12 000 miles away in England:

> When you're unemployed, it's as though you're not a person, as though you're not entitled to have any ideas. Often when I'm talking in a pub, sooner or later it gets around to, 'What sort of job do you do?' and if you say you're unemployed, that's it: end of conversation! It's as though your opinions aren't worth knowing.[10]

The response to this ostracism is the kind of retreat into isolation which Bill refered to earlier. Bill and his friends are caught in a vicious circle where their poverty forces them into a physical ghetto like the barracks they live in. Similarly, their low self-esteem, their drug taking, and the community ostracism forces them into a social ghetto. Both make getting a job and regaining self-esteem even more difficult.

In turn, this further promotes the retreat into the privatised, aimless existence:

Bob: When you get a job you just feel a better person. You feel like standing up to the world, and just sort of walking into it, but when you're on the dole you just back away from the whole world. Fucking half the time you think, 'Oh fuck, I don't want to go outside today. I'll keep me door fast'.
Bill: Half the time you're hidden away.

Traditionally, mass unemployment has politically fragmented the working class, undermined its solidarity by setting up one group of workers, the employed, against another, the unemployed. When Bill and Andy indulge in a spate of union bashing, they follow this pattern. Here they give vent to their resentment at being denied work and their jealousy towards those 'lucky enough' to have work:

Bill: When you're on the dole and you hear about some of the strikes that go on, you just laugh, it's just stupidity.
Andy: Cause you think, we're here starving and they're fucking not working for about three months and go back to work and get paid for it. Why can't they just sack the fucking lot of them and put everyone else on.
Bill: Just because they don't get pink-coloured toilet paper they have a strike for it.
IW: What, you think cause these people are lucky enough to be working they should be...
Andy: Fucking work, that's it.
Bill: Well I believe, you know, the harder you work, the more you should get. You know, you work for your money. If you don't work for your money you shouldn't get it.
Andy: Like all that garbage in Melbourne piling up. We're sitting here, fucking hanging out for food and they're fucking just turning down jobs. Why can't they just fuck the lot of them off and get the unemployed people, not just the unemployed, but just hire a whole new staff. It's not that hard, they reckon there's so many fucking unemployed. Why can't they just sack the lot of them. Bang. Hire new peole. I've had jobs that do that. You say 'Boo' to them and that's it, they sack you, cause they know they can get someone straight away.
Bill: Like if you walk up to someone who's been on the dole for a while, and say, 'Listen, I've got a job for you, a labouring job. It pays, say, a hundred and eighty a week'. You know he goes, 'Oh right oh, take me'. And you know, he'll work and he'll be satisfied for what he's getting and you'll find he won't complain like people that's never been on the dole. They just whinge and complain and that. But if you say put them on the dole for about a year and a half or so, you'll find they won't be striking like they used to.

When Bill voices the ethos of working hard—'If you don't work for your money you shouldn't get it'—he is actually condemning himself. The logic of his argument is that he, as someone out of work, should not get an income. The reason for this contradictory judgment is that, in this passage, Bill is looking at the world through the eyes of the bosses, not the workers.

The unemployed have always provided a reserve army for the bosses, a large mass of docile workers ready to strike break, ready to undercut award wages, desperate for work on any terms. This is exactly what happens in Andy's example where the bosses use the existence of high unemployment to control their workers:

> You say 'Boo' to them and that's it, they sack you, cause they know they can get someone straight away.

and

> if you put them on the dole for about a year and a half or so, you'll find they won't be striking like they used to.

When Andy admits that workers have no rights on some jobs, he clearly perceives that the pool of unemployed people provide the bosses with power. But this is not seen as powerlessness on his part, because he does not identify with the workers. He seems to identify with the bosses, and their rule is law: the workers only 'whinge' and 'complain', and, as for the unions, they're the 'stirrers' behind it all. As the unemployed in this scenario, Bill and Andy are grateful for the opportunity to work and thus allegiance goes to the providers of work, not to their fellow workers.

Bill and his friends are not only divided from the working class at the workplace, but this division carries over into their leisure. In terms of their daily activities, Bill and his friends aspire toward working-class leisure patterns, an existence well beyond their dole incomes:

> On the dole you just can't rage at all, but if you don't rage at all you just get so bored...and to try and do all the normal things on the dole which is virtually impossible, you've got to starve. It's sorta feast then famine, feast then famine, and that's how it is you know.

This excerpt explains one of the observations commonly made by youth workers. They note how young people 'blow their dole cheque' in the first few days and then have no money for the last week of their fortnight. No doubt this problem is compounded by poor training in money management, but it is mainly due to the need for psychological survival. The unemployed want to lead normal lives, they want to escape this ostracism and isolation. Leading 'normal lives' means trying to match the lifestyles of their peers in the workforce. Finally, there's sometimes just the need to life your spirits. As Debbie, another long-term unemployed person, put it:

> You don't get much extravaganza things in your life so I make the most of my cheque.

Bill and his friends are also fragmented in ways that run deeper than their current situation. They are fragmented along gender lines, divided from their female peers by a set of deeply rooted sexist attitudes and practices. Not only do Bill and his friends espouse sexist sentiments in the conversation, but from the comments of several youth workers it is apparent that they relate to their female acquaintances in sexist ways.

At one stage the conversation touched on the predicament of being an unemployed woman. Bill expressed some sympathy towards women in this plight but this was soon exploded by Bob's sexist outburst:

> *Bill*: From the way I look at it I reckon the unemployed women have got it heaps worse cause you know like if you can't really sorta protect yourself and look after yourself that well when you're a woman on the dole, then that's just really bad. A lot of unemployed women get really put down, you know, they get called moles and sluts.
> *Bob*: Yeah, yeah, that's how it mostly is.
> *IW*: Why's that?
> *Bill*: Mainly cause they're unemployed. They're sorta easy going and because they're easy going, sorta, that's mainly due to the dole I suppose...if a chick dressed cheaply she gets classed, STAMP: 'You're a mole.' That's it. Most of them anyway.
> *Bob*: Well a lot of them are like that. [Pause] Thank god for that. [General laughter]

The picture of fragmentation and disunity is now complete. As unemployed working-class youths, Bill and his friends are divided from the employed working class both at the workplace and in their leisure. Even within the ranks of unemployed, there is the further division along gender lines. In a way, the exploitation of unemployed women by these men is a kind of compensatory mechanism: because the oppressed men are offered another group to oppress, their anger against their own condition is blunted.

Indeed, this is one of the most disturbing features of the lifestyle of Bill and his friends: there is no political outcry against their oppression, no rebellion against their condition.

Why is this so? What prevents large numbers of unemployed teenagers taking to the streets and demanding an end to their hopeless existence?

For a start, the fragmentation and disunity outlined above prevents the kind of solidarity which a mass movement must gain if its members are to feel confident. To this can be added the numbing effects of hunger, poverty and homelessness. These material conditions crush people like Bill and his friends into a privatised ghetto. The most their resentment mobilises them for is petty theft, not political protest. Bill dryly notes: 'Well, dole means poverty and poverty means stealing and so on.' Bob adds: 'Poverty means you've got to rip off things to sell them.'

Again, the diagnosis determines the solution. All these youths recognise their poverty; they know that others have jobs and wealth, and they don't. However, they do not see this in structural terms, as a situation determined by the way the society is organised around the profit motive, an arrangement whereby a decreasing minority get richer at the expense of the majority. Rather, Bill and his friends focus on the surface features, the fact that some people own things and others don't. Political activity aimed at structural changes to bring about a redistribution of wealth is not part of the panorama in which they move. Their landscape is one where this person or that person has wealth and theft is the means for its redistribution:

> *Bill*: If I was out to steal it'd only be just to make me survive, just survive. Like I wouldn't steal off anybody who was worse off than me... I'd rip something off someone that's rich and it just doesn't matter to them.

When I posed the question of redistribution of wealth as an answer to poverty, I received the following responses:

> *IW*: When you see rich people like that, do you feel you want to be rich like them...
> *Bill*: Oh yeah, you have your dreams...

IW: ...or do you think, 'No one should be rich, we should all be the same'.
Bill: Oh you're looking at communism if everyone's just the same.
Bob: I wouldn't look at it that way.
IW: You just want to be rich like them?
Bob: No not even that. I wouldn't look at it any of those two ways that you said.
IW: How would you look at it?
Bob: Just mind me own business.
IW: But you'd get angry wouldn't you?
Bob: Oh yeah, when you get drunk you get a little bit angry.

In trying to understand why Bill and his friends are so politically powerless it is important to stress the features of the wider society as well as the unique features of their condition.

Political activity in contemporary society has largely been removed from the province of ordinary people. Representative democracy and government by bureaucracy demand of people only a few minutes of their time in a ballot box every few years. This relieves people of any obligation to participate in a routine and direct manner in the political processes which determine their lives. People are neither trained nor given the openings to make those political decisions which would allow them to control their own lives more fully. This is reinforced by the conduct of political discussion, which can be so mystifying that ordinary people are simply excluded from fruitful involvement. Jurgen Habermas has convincingly argued that politics has been increasingly removed from the realm of 'practical knowledge' (in which all could partake) and has become located within the realm of 'technical knowledge' (in which only experts can speak).[11] This change is reflected in the modern sense of the word 'politics'. It is identified almost exclusively with the narrow sense of power broking ('party politics', 'it was a political decision', and so on) rather than with the fuller sense: the power to make decisions about controlling one's life and participating directly in making decisions about the organisation of social life.

The way the media deals with politics does not make it more accessible, but on the contrary, removes it even further from people's control. The media trivialises political discussion and reduces its structural features to a crude clash of 'personalities'. Not only does this cement individualism into yet another niche of daily life but it profoundly robs political discussion of any potential analytical value. When Bill and his friends directed their anger toward the government for its part in causing their plight, their focus stayed on the level of personalities:

IW: You said before the government was partly to blame for unemployment?
Bob: Fraser's a prick.
[General laughter]
Bill: When you're on the dole, they all are.
Bob: He goes on, 'Gonna do this' when the election's on. 'We'll do this for unemployment we'll do that.' But they do fuck-all for the unemployed.

Bill: Fraser's saying, 'Tighten your belt. Just hang in there and we'll work it out'. I suppose that's not too bad cause if you just sort of hang in there, and stay with what you've got, things might get better. But everyone's just striking and no one wants to do that. They just want to get better and more money.
IW: But that sort of hang in there is also meant to be for you people, hang around and stay unemployed until something turns up. I mean, it's not going to is it?
Bill: Hmm. [Shrugs]
IW: Would it make any difference if Hayden [then leader of the Labor opposition] was in?
Bob: I don't know. I'm not much into politics. I wouldn't go near it. All I know is it sucks.

Bob's comment sums up well the total sense of estrangement which parliamentary politics produces for powerless people like himself.

There is a danger with a book like this, which deals with how people think, that readers will draw the conclusion that if only people thought differently, then the society would be different. This is a highly misleading conclusion to draw because it ignores why people come to think the way they do. As all the chapters in this book will show, the social conditions which determine people's lives also determine their ideas. It is these social conditions, for Bill and his friends, their unemployment, their poverty and their homelessness, which must be overcome before their dignity and self-esteem can return. Political changes aimed at providing the unemployed with satisfying and worthwhile work, a secure standard of living, and adequate provision of housing are the answers to the plight of people like Bill and his friends.

If these changes can come through grassroots political activism, then so much the better. Such activism returns to the unemployed a sense of purpose, a structure to their days, a chance to reconstruct their dignity. Most importantly, political activism channels their anger and their frustrations outwards. It prevents that anger festering inside and fermenting all the psychological symptoms which this chapter has illustrated.

In England in the 1930s, unemployed women and men set out from the most depressed areas of the country to march on London and protest at their deplorable living conditions. Along the way, thousands joined these 'Hunger Marches' and eventually massive crowds converged on London's Hyde Park.

The unemployed refused to stay hidden away. Their marching mobilised the working people of England behind their cause. For the unemployed themselves, the marches brought a new sense of purpose to their lives. As one Jarrow hunger marcher declared:

> The fine thing is knowing that when we get up in the mornings there's something worthwhile to do.[12]

3
'The door's always open'

Gail: It's a thing you're never meant to say because being on the dole is disgusting, but this place [an alternative school] does prepare people for living on the dole a lot better than any other school cause it just teaches you how to live, how to live and not to need something, and to be self-determining. You do something because *you* want to, that kind of stuff...

As well as the long-term unemployed, like Bill and his friends, I also spoke with another group of unemployed youths. These were the 'transitory unemployed', whose dole experiences were measured in months rather than years. These were middle-class youths who had completed their secondary education and for whom tertiary study or working careers remained an option.

The unemployed middle class has not been spared the confrontation with the dole bludger stigma:

Maria: I didn't like having to say that I was unemployed because that seems like the only thing you do. 'What are you?' 'I'm unemployed.' Well I'm not. You know I do plenty of stuff. I'm very busy, I'm very keen to learn and to do different things. And I hated it, that that's what was attached to me: 'Maria Rinaldo Unemployed'...

While people like Maria confront this stigma in the community at large, on a more personal level of family and friends there is a supportive empathy for the predicament for being jobless. Claudia, who is also unemployed, has parents who endorse whatever she decides to put her energies into:

Claudia: My dad is behind me whatever I do and just very supportive and caring and all the rest, so he doesn't say, 'You should do that. You shouldn't do that'. He goes, 'It's good Claudia'.

This marks a strong contrast with Bill's father, encountered in the last chapter. Such family rejection meant long periods of homelessness and destitution for people like Bill and his friends. For people like Maria and Claudia, there is this strong family support, and also the companionship of a large friendship network, the legacy of their recent schooling.

Charles, who attends the same alternative school as Gail, was unemployed for a year at the end of fourth form. Despite leaving at the age when Bill and his friends did, however, the reactions he received from other people were different once they knew he intended to return to school:

Charles: I had a few problems... I told people I met that I finished school in fourth form and sort of it's hard to describe but I could sorta feel that they were thinking, 'Oh he's one of them that leaves school in fourth form'.

And I said, 'But I'm going to go back to school next year'. And that made it alright, so I didn't have too many problems that way because they knew it was only temporary.

During this period Charles did find a job, only to find how alienating the world of work can be:

Charles: I really hated the way it was all plastic and metal and there were no windows in the store. Just go in there, work all day, being told what to do in a really nasty way by the boss.

. . .

It wasn't particularly boring. But it would have got boring after a while. And I hated just being in this little building, you know, not being able to go outside at all, and also the authoritarian side of things, I didn't like that a lot. Also I didn't like the idea of the way it seemed it was going to stretch into the future. They were all, even in those first two days, they were getting me thinking about a career at Woolworths you know, that sort of thing.
IW: Why is that such a horrible prospect?
Charles: Oh gees, two days was... I mean a career selling that rubbishy stuff, I just couldn't stand it, it'd be just totally unsatisfying and revolting.

. . .

Also it was a lot to do with just going inside all day and being away from nature. Like I'd get up in the morning before it got light and sorta go to work and come home after the sun had gone down.
IW: What kind of changes would have been necessary to keep you there?
Charles: Well they would have had to get rid of that guy in charge, put a few windows in the store, made it smaller and thrown out all the rubbish I was selling. Which was shoes and I don't think there was one leather one in the whole shop. They were all plastic.
IW: You resented selling shoddy stuff?

Charles: Yeah. It's just totally unsatisfying. You know you sell someone these shoes that you know are going to fall apart in about five minutes... I'd like to sell things that I know are going to last for a while and are worth having and not feel as if I'm ripping people off.

At the end of that year, Charles returned to finish his secondary education. He enrolled at an alternative school and now, with only a few weeks before the end of his final term, Charles speculates about being on the dole again. In the last chapter it was clear that Andy's school experiences had totally disillusioned him with further education. With Charles, there is the complete opposite:

Charles: The problem that I see with being on the dole is just becoming sorta apathetic. Like I want to do things, like I want to keep learning after leaving school about the sort of things we learn here. I'd like to investigate maths a lot more, science and all sorts of things. If I could keep doing that sort of thing then I'd be able to keep out of this apathetic stuff. The idea is just to keep your mind active.

Charles extends this axiom to cover his body as well. He is now regularly involved in a range of outdoor recreations: cycling, bushwalking, and cross-country skiing. These activities are accompanied by a strong environmental awareness. Charles' schooling introduced him to all these activities and it also contained many environmentally oriented subjects in its curriculum. Throughout the course of our conversation, Charles would often employ concrete environmental problems in his references to abstract issues being discussed.

The last time I saw Charles he was wheeling his pushbike beside a group of friends. They were all marching in one of the large Palm Sunday peace rallies which have become a major political event during the last few years.

The legacy of Charles' schooling is very different from that of Bill and his friends. Charles has gained an enthusiasm for learning and at the same time he has acquired a range of practical skills which allow him to fill his hours with enriching activities. One obvious result of this is that he can feel good about himself and can keep his self-esteem intact.

Maria is in a similar situation. Not only do her options for further study remain open, but the legacy of her schooling has been equally positive in terms of self-esteem:

Maria: Yeah, see for us, we've chosen not to go to uni. We've chosen not to do certain things. But the door's always open. We

always know we can succeed in terms of this world. We know that
when we choose to, it's right there. And so I go on, I know I can get
As, I know I can get Bs, and I know I can succeed: socially, financially,
or whatever. I've just got a positive outlook because of that, and I like
myself and all the rest of it. That's all helped to mould that and give
me that feeling. That I'm OK, that I can choose to do what I want,
because I'm in the upper stream of people.

Clearly, having a door always open, rather than being locked into the dole spiral as are Bill and his friends, is a major factor in the psychological survival which Charles, Maria and Claudia achieve. As well as this, they feel good about themselves and find support among family and friends, and as well as this, they have a critical attitude toward the society around them. Charles is very sensitive to the environmentally destructive nature of capitalist society; Claudia and Maria are strongly aware of the oppressive nature of the patriarchal society they live in. The critical stances which each of these people adopt serve as insurance policies against self-denigration. Being critical allows them to focus their frustrations outward and to minimise that negative self-absorption which can so easily swamp the unemployed. Certainly, there are periods of depression for these people, but their gaze is far more outward than inward.

This is well illustrated in the case of Gail. She is eighteen years old and unemployed. In front of her lies a prospective university course, behind her a supportive family and friendship network. As a young girl Gail grew up in a socialist family: her parents were active in the sixties anti-war movement. Later her mother became a strong feminist and also developed a close involvement with alternative schools. Gail herself has spent four years in alternative schools, institutions which embody the spiritual values of the sixties counter-cultural movement.

This background permeates her thinking. She has a perceptive understanding of the nature of capitalism, a finely tuned sensitivity to her spiritual needs, and, integrating everything into an overall perspective, a strong feminist outlook.

Gail sees sexism as far more than just a question of discrimination:

> I think sexism's everywhere. It's in all of us and it's really deeply
> rooted, and I've started to see especially lately, that males and
> females are incredibly divided, they're almost like different species

and

men don't bond very satisfactorily to each other in a meaningful way and therefore really need women as a source of nurturing and love and all that sort of human understanding, for self-respect and so on. They need to keep women controlled so that they have, like any other commodity, a good supply of it. Keep women in the home so that they will always be there to give it to them when they want it.

Gail also perceives how men, in being locked into stereotyped masculinities, are also oppressed by sexism:

In a way I think that men are in a really fucked situation. They're a lot worse off than women because women have got, what we've been engendered into is really compassionate, nurturing skills and when we turn to each other to do that, we're a lot better off and in a lot of ways we're a lot stronger.

The comparison is a useful one for Gail, but she does not let it blind her to how much women are the real victims of sexism:

Being put down all the time and having your body objectified. And being given shit jobs and having really low self-esteem. Like there's a lot of really horrible things about the way women are treated... but it's in different areas.

When Gail turns to consider the questions of schooling and the world of work, she brings to bear all the force of her insights into the nature of capitalism:

I think that schools are used as a training ground to dull feelings. I did a unit called 'Inside Classrooms' where we went around to all different schools and sat in on classes. And just again and again I got this feeling of everybody sitting there... and everything gets dulled and numb and shut off and so I see that as a training for jobs where there's that mindless, nothing kind of existence that goes on for hours. And that's what school is. That's a major instrument for conditioning the human beings that come into the society and squashing all their spontaneous, colourful being.

Gail pursues this criticism of work under capitalism, focusing in particular on the division of labour. She argues for both industrial democracy and for income redistribution:

Imagine if they could get everyone to take turns doing the different jobs. Still if it wasn't really good fun it'd at least be interesting and you'd learn to do lots of other things. They could just do it so much better.

and

> They should scale people's incomes according to how many children they've got, and what their needs are, and not to the value that their work is given. I mean, maybe people who do really shit factory jobs should be given more money than people who do enjoyable thinking jobs.

Gail is well aware that this is unlikely to happen and notes eloquently why factory workers do in fact get lower wages:

> Because they're easily replaceable. They're just unskilled worker units. There's millions of them. They don't need that person for that person, they just need them for their arms that move, and there's plenty of arms that move. They're not worth much.

Gail's own approach to a job has evolved from a childhood idealism into a gradual awareness of the real meaning of work:

> When I was young I always believed that there would be a job for me that I would enjoy and that would be meaningful and worthwhile. And I guess that was just because of my family and I just believed that's how it happened. I didn't have much concept of how shitty jobs can be.

Yet to some extent she has kept her ideal intact, still defining the perfect job in these terms:

> I want to feel like it's part of my personal direction, my evolving and unfolding as I read and think and go through ideas and images. And if my work were something like that, where it were part of my real, living being, that's growing and changing, that'd be really good.

The ideology which lies behind Gail's socialist perspective and her views on personal creativity is the spiritual ethos of the 1960s counter-culture.[13] This ideology was the inspiration at the heart of her progressive schooling, and many of her present friends live alternative lifestyles.

In the same way that the 1960s generation discovered that the values of creativity and spiritual fulfilment could only be realised by 'dropping out', Gail believes that in the 1980s it is probably only on the dole that such creativity and spiritual living can be pursued. She has high esteem for the unemployed:

> The other day we were talking about how the unemployed people are doing the most worthwhile job in society. Which is doing all the thinking and dealing with existential loneliness that nobody else dares tackle. And being poets and creative and just dealing with all that other side of things which is really valuable.

This understanding makes it easy for Gail to contemplate a worthwhile life on the dole for herself:

> I think it'd be really nice on the dole. I feel like I've got a kind of community of people who are on the dole and who live a really constructive, creative sort of life. And I think that's such a valuable thing to do. Something without the sort of outside whip over you, saying you've got to do this and giving you that incentive of pleasing someone else. It's just sort of YOU who says, 'OK get up and do it', and you do it.

Working through her ideas is not something Gail has had to do in isolation. As well as the stimulus of her school subjects and the conversations with her peers, there is the impact of her family and her older friends. This last group counts for a lot:

> I give them a lot of power as in values. Like when they say something it really hits home. I really think about it and sometimes I find that really hard because I don't want to think like what they've said. But it happens because they're so important to me.

When Gail voices her sentiments about living on the dole, she finds a certain resistance to the idea on the part of these older friends:

> Those people who are really important to me, when I'd sorta say, 'I can't wait to be on the dole, so I can stop being dependent on my parents'. And they'd say, 'Why don't you, ha, ha, try and get a job, try for something higher'. As if it is higher. But it did make it seem like more acceptance of work. Their way of thinking, work is what you do.

Consequently, Gail concluded her discussion about a future dole life by alluding to recent thoughts about entering the Public Service. When I indicated scepticism about creative fulfilment in that area, she responded, half-laughing, 'You do it when you get home'. Despite the flippancy here, this response does point to a serious tension in her thinking. Gail is not prepared to renounce entirely her idealisation of dole living, yet she has begun to move towards what she calls 'a degree of acceptance' of stultifying work.

Eight months after this conversation I met Gail again. She had spent a period of about six months on the dole followed by a brief time in paid employment. All this while she had also been working as a volunteer childcare worker at a women's refuge. I turned on the tape recorder and we picked up the threads of our last conversation.

Gail was happy for the opportunity to reflect upon her recent experiences of work and I was interested to see if the tensions in her life which I had glimpsed before were still there. The main tension I had seen was between Gail's search for personal fulfilment through creativity and her need for security and recognition through employment. In a way, it was a question of the rivalry between the spiritual ideology of the counter-culture and the ideology of 'middle-class respectability' (that is, the pressure to carve out a career path with its material security).

Gail's family background has offered the vision of a working life based on principles of creative self-fulfilment. Her grandfather was an academic; both her mother and her father are teachers and writers. Within Gail's family, therefore, the tensions between creativity and respectability have been resolved by success in the right kinds of jobs.

In a recession, however, with a tight labour market, a matriculation certificate means that all that Gail can hope for are those same boring, stultifying jobs which she castigates. Under these conditions, the tension between rival ideologies is very great indeed: either Gail follows the path of creativity and accepts the insecurity of dole living, or she accepts the respectability of a job which is meaningless and alienating. (The other option, university study, is the one which Gail eventually adopts, but I will talk about this later.)

As her earlier comments have shown, while still at school, Gail favoured the idea of rejecting the prospect of labour-market entry, and its stultifying consequences, and instead emphasised the potential creativity of the dole. After leaving school, this is what happened:

> I had all the assumptions that there would be a job for me. I don't think my thing was so much that there are jobs for people who want them and that if you work hard enough—oh, I guess I did have that. I sort of felt like, that if I really wanted one, and I just tried, and tried and I looked and looked, I would get one. But also it was a lot based on my belief in myself as being different and special. You know and I'm a really wonderful person therefore there'll be a job for me, you know. Sort of tying those two up.
>
> And I started out writing applications for jobs in the uni library and things like that and I sort of wrote them and I didn't do anything too

immediate. Sort of go and see people or anything where I might start working the next day. I was just sort of happy with that for a few months then in about April I'd had enough of that and I'd decided that I would go and start looking for a job, sort of going around asking people.

I'd sort of got a bit more realistic by this time. I'd sort of started realising...I'd sort of stopped applying for jobs cause I thought, 'Oh look, there's no way I'm going to get it'. And that was really hard cause like having equated my personal worth with my getting a job, that started to really get me down.

Like I guess I did then but I do now in a more realistic way believe in work. Like the need to do some sort of work and be doing something. And what I was saying is that I really respect people who can live on the dole and do work and make their own work and live satisfactorily like that.

I suppose I knew because the people lived with while I was at school didn't do that. They seemed to be happy but they weren't doing any meaningful work and they were living very much on that pleasure-oriented, floating, you know, 'Do whatever comes up. No commitment' sort of thing which I don't like. And I suppose that I did that for a while when I left school. I'd seen them doing it and I thought I'd like that and I wanted to get away from having to go to school so I did that for a while.

But sort of even then I knew that I wouldn't want to do it for very long. There was that thing of always people asking you what you are doing and I'd have to say something respectable, you know, like I'm applying for jobs. Because of all the cultural stuff that's really deep within me somewhere, that to work is to be worthwhile and that it is shameful to be unemployed. And that it's even shameful to be working at something you're not paid for, you know it's somehow less. And so there has been within me somewhere the need to work for those reasons.... Also there became the need for money...

There's also the thing that I believe that work is like identifying myself as a revolutionary sort of person. That it's really satisfying and worthwhile to be working within the community or be working anywhere to be able to be subversive and to have some hand in changing things and that to do that you need to be there. So there's some part of that in it too and that's reflected in the sort of work that I've chosen. That's happening more lately. While I was looking for jobs in the library it wasn't that, it was sort of much more typically oriented reasons.

The tension between middle-class respectability and spiritual fulfilment is strikingly apparent in this passage. Gail's initial involvement with the counter-culture-style dole existence has been eclipsed by a reassertion of her middle-class values. This happens partly for economic reasons—'there became the need for money'—and also because of cultural conditioning: 'it's shameful to be unemployed.' The creativity which was meant to accompany living on the dole also failed to materialise fully. Instead there was a kind of aimlessness: 'that floating..."whatever comes up, no commitment sort of thing" which I don't like.'

Finally, Gail is aware that dole living can be a form of escapism: dropping out from an alienating world of work means also dropping out of the possibilities for political intervention. At this point in her reflections, Gail has focused on the socialist elements in her outlook. This perspective provides the rationale not for deserting the world of work, but for making a more vigorous entry: 'to have some hand in changing things...you have to be there.'

During her period of unemployment, Gail's vulnerability to the ideology of middle-class respectability grew increasingly stronger:

> It's important to me that I can write out proper job applications, five-page job applications, get dressed up in the right sort of clothes and go and talk to them. And I can be successful in that way and it's important to me and I mean that's part of my image of myself as a middle-class daughter. And I've had a lot of you know, 'you're wonderful' sort of stuff put on me from my mother, but also from my grandfather who would respect that sort of thing. And so that worldly success is important to me on some level. I mean I can write the applications and they like me and all that sort of stuff.

This recognition of her middle-class values does not amount to a sell-out because Gail is still as politically committed as before. She still knows what the world of work represents, but she now has a better understanding of her own vulnerability. She now knows how important to her is the social recognition which a job brings and of how hard it is to find any jobs, let alone satisfying ones. For Gail this makes it necessary to come to terms with the ideology of middle-class respectability and to reject the lure of an idealised dole life. This has not meant a rejection of the values of creativity, self-fulfilment and autonomy because these are still reflected in the kinds of work Gail continues to seek—jobs which involve working with children for example.

In fact, Gail eventually finds a job at a handicapped children's centre. She brings to this job all her political awareness and all the insights into the issues of autonomy and respect for people which her own schooling highlighted for her. However, Gail quickly discovers how out of place they are:

> I went to the handicapped children's centre and actually did get a job from going and asking them. And they actually fired me. The woman who employs everybody said it had turned out I wasn't suitable and that she had to keep her staff happy and that I was a very nice person but that I didn't have enough experience.
>
> And so I thought, 'OK I'm going to ask these people and get some feedback on this'. And we were working away and it was the last night I was going to be there and we could all talk about it but one of them got me and took me into the office and made the kids in there go away. They're like that. And said, 'You're too idealistic and you don't understand why we do these things'.
>
> I mean it was basically that they could feel that I disapproved of some of the ways they worked. It just really unsettled them, it was uncomfortable for them and they couldn't do any questioning so it had to be me who sort of didn't understand why you have to be like this and that I was just unexperienced and I should go out in the world and you know come to terms with reality and then I'd be alright. [Half laughs] So I didn't feel too bad about that.
>
> Oh, they'd yell at the kids, you know. They were good and they cared and they had relationships with the children. They treated some of the adults there, there were some who were about twenty, as children. When they wanted them to do something they just used their power as adults, shouting or threatening to get them to do it. They weren't looking at why the child was doing what they want to do. They could just feel my, I mean, I didn't even say anything. I guess just with my face... I'd talk to the kids, someone would ask me if they could do something and I'd say 'Yes' and it'd turn out it was against the rules. A few times my way of relating to them as people meant that the others were losing their grip. And it just unsettled it.

When Gail was at school, the administration meetings which ran the school involved both teachers and students relating as equals. Among the teachers there was no official hierarchy—no principal or deputies—and as far as was feasible, decisions were made on the basis of participatory democracy. The stress all the time was on treating students as people and respecting their autonomy. Consequently, Gail views this children's centre through the eyes of her own schooling. It measures up very poorly:

> took me into the office and made the kids in there go away. They're like that... when they wanted them to do something they just used their power as adults, shouting or threatening to get them to do it. They weren't looking at why the child was doing what they wanted to

do...my way of relating to them as people meant that the others were losing their grip.

Clearly, Gail's political awareness has made her a very subversive person. She has entered a workplace where deference to hierarchies is expected, where innovation from those lower in the hierarchy is frowned upon, where unequal power relations are entrenched. All of this means that Gail's democratic practices are a real threat to the official ideology of the place. Not surprisingly, she is sacked.

Gail's political outlook has brought her back on to the dole again. But at the same time it has strongly protected her sense of self-worth. In no way does Gail regard her dismissal as a slight against herself. She clearly perceives that the fault lies with the nature of the institution:

> It was uncomfortable for them and they couldn't do any questioning so it had to be me who sort of didn't understand why you have to be like this and that I was just unexperienced and I should go out into the world and you know come to terms with reality and then I'd be alright. [Half laughs] So I didn't feel too bad about that.

Not only has Gail seen through the sham of blaming her for being 'unexperienced' but she can even understand why they adopt this position. She knows that they need to blame her in order not to have to a look at what is wrong with their own institution.

Throughout Gail's whole analysis, individualism is absent. Indeed it is in retreat. Gail almost aggressively focuses on the structures responsible for the outcomes. She refuses to see herself as the 'problem', and she does not even see the other workers in the centre as at fault: 'They were good and they cared.' Gail sees the workers, like the children, as equally trapped into a set of structures which imprison them in destructive forms of interaction.

For Gail this whole experience has been very positive. She has lost a job, but she remains confident that she was doing the right thing. Her political awareness and her faith in being subversive mean that places like the children's centre have become a challenge:

> I've been to a training workshop with them [another handicapped centre] and I'm just finding there's virtually going to be no one who

thinks or feels the way I do and that's going to be really hard. But I sort of feel really challenged to work there, in those places with those people. If I've got all these ideas and these ways of being, I feel like I need more experience to show that they work and feel more confident in them. To be able to really confront the other people with them.

Another legacy of Gail's schooling is that she possesses the means to rise to this challenge. She has both the confidence to deal with her isolation and also the skills of self-learning with which to strengthen her position:

I can do this stuff with the handicapped and I'm a lot more challenged by that cause I've had to do a lot of thinking. I've had to start reading about behaviour modification so I can argue with people about it.

As it turned out, Gail did not return to working in handicapped centres but instead took up university studies. This is no surprise: the option was always there. The tension between, on the one hand, creative fulfilling work, and on the other hand, respectability and security, is rarely resolved. There is one area, however, where respectability and fulfilment often coincide: university studies. This gains the approving nod from the ideology of middle-class respectability, and university also avoids the boredom and alienation which comes from entry into the world of work.

The way Gail has pursued this option is again distinctive and reflects her particular background. She chose a university whose course structure was closest to that of her school in terms of student control over learning, and is now studying a course on social and political theory in a department where students are encouraged to integrate their studies into an overall perspective. In Gail's case this has meant feminism.

Gail may have followed the 'typical middle-class' road, she may have left her idealised dole existence behind her, but the direction her future is heading bears strong witness to the power of her political outlook and the fruitful legacy of her progressive schooling.

Part II
The Peer Group and the Family

4
The peer group as a battlefield

> Running away, I'd never thought of doing that. You know, you've seen it on TV, people running away from home and they always get back and it's all love and that's it. When I ran away from home it felt like hell because I felt like I couldn't go back. I found it's a big black hole out there. And you had to be careful of all the cars that went past cause I ran away in the nightime and I was scared and I thought I might get raped.

Lucy pauses to light another cigarette, the eighth since the conversation began. Her voice sounds hoarse and she coughs intermittently. Lucy has been sick lately and at one point leaves the room to take some medication.

Four of us are sitting in the living room a four-bedroom suburban house: Lucy, Janet, Stuart and myself. The house is not an ordinary dwelling: one of the rooms is a small office and the other three are filled with bunks for twelve people. We are in a youth refuge where Stuart is one of the youth workers and Lucy and Janet are residents.

This refuge bears witness to the massive increase in youth homelessness over the last decade. Like so many of the other refuges springing up in Australian cities, it serves the needs of young people who are desperate for shelter. Many of the unemployed residents have been thrown out of home by intolerant parents who are convinced 'there's work for those who want it' and cannot come to terms with their children's unemployment. Other residents have left country towns for the city, lured by the hope of a job. They soon find themselves in the vicious circle of itinerant dole poverty where a place like this is a real refuge from sleeping under bridges or in parked cars. Pinned to the noticeboard in the refuge office is a small newspaper clipping:

> It's hardly the Ritz, but at least it's warm. A lad resident at the local youth refuge said on Friday that he, and many others he knew, had

recently been forced to sleep in charity clothing bins around town because they had nowhere else to go. It was a bit claustrophobic, he said, but sometimes the metal flap could be propped open with donated clothes to allow in air.

The refuge is also a temporary home for young people who have run away from home: from parents separating, from violent parents, or from personal problems which are compounded by family life. For these young people, the refuge provides a temporary breathing space, a quiet time to unwind.

I have mentioned already that the people in this book are not a representative sample. This is particularly so for this chapter. In dealing with the question of the peer group, I present only the experiences of a few young women and I deal only with heterosexual relationships. Despite these limitations this chapter still offers valuable insights into the psychological processes which underlie sexual relations and, most importantly, the power relations which structure those sexual relations.

Lucy, nevertheless, is fairly typical of the young working-class women who have run away from home and who end up in the refuge. Both she and Janet have left home because of continual conflicts with their parents. The issue at heart was invariably the question of how much social freedom they were to be allowed. This is how Lucy puts it:

> I was going out with blokes, All of a sudden my mum thought I was growing up too fast. My dad used to call me a little baby, he still does: 'His little baby.' And all of a sudden, I turned around and said, 'I'm sixteen now'. And my dad thought, 'Gawd, she's growing up, she'll be moving out of home, getting married, having kids'. All this just hit him and then they sorta locked me up.
>
> I wasn't allowed to go out or anything. And I always like to go out and meet people and have fun and when this happened I thought, 'What the hell have I done wrong to stay home?'
>
> But for a couple of months I wasn't allowed out at all, except to go to school. And I thought, 'Christ. I must have done something really bad', and mum wouldn't tell me.
>
> And she thought I was going to marry this bloke I was going out with, and he had a car and everything. And I was getting to be a real big girl. And then mum started hating him. I wouldn't be home much and one day it dawned on them. I was getting there...and they just wanted me to stay at home and be a good little girl and sit down and read bookies and things like that and play with jigsaw puzzles. [Laughs]

> And then when I left home I think that really broke my mum's heart because she wanted me to stay there and be a little girl still. But now that I've left home I think she's worked out that I'm capable of looking after myself. That's the thing that I wanted to show them. That I can be independent if I want to. Like leaving home and staying out of trouble and that sort of thing. Which I have.

It is worth looking closely at the way Lucy views this episode, particularly the interpretation she gives of herself and of her parents' perceptions of her. Lucy is very concerned to depict herself as a mature adult, someone who is 'capable of looking after myself' and able to 'stay out of trouble'. Her parents, however, are unable to recognise this and treat her as a child.

Lucy presents this interpretation very skilfully. She makes use of selective evidence: 'My dad used to call me a little baby.' She conjures up emotive images, some of which are almost parody: 'read bookies...and play with jigsaw puzzles.' She even projects particular motives on to her parents in order to reinforce her interpretation: 'my dad thought, "Gawd, she's growing up ...getting married".' The whole episode is thus presented as a situation where unreasonable restrictions were placed on her freedom. For Lucy her parents did this, not because of concern for her welfare, but because they are afraid she is growing up too fast. In Lucy's eyes, her parents motives are selfish and their outlook is narrow-minded. Lucy sees herself as someone who is maturing rapidly: 'he had a car and everything. I was getting to be a real big girl.' And she sees her parents as people who cannot come to terms with this process.

Maturity means several things to Lucy. It represents responsibility for making decisions and looking after herself: 'That I can be independent if I want to.' When Lucy is 'locked up', her parents are not simply restricting Lucy's social life; they are also denying this image of maturity to which Lucy holds so firmly.

If family conflict is understood in this way, as a battle about being accepted by others as one sees oneself, then it is easier to understand the following passages. In these Lucy and Janet are discussing their social life and they consistently argue that they should be allowed the freedom to look after themselves, the freedom to express their maturity. Notice below how they employ a 'self' and 'other' distinction and that the 'other' is a hypothetical 18-year-old, someone who had been locked up and denied freedom in her social life:

Lucy: I reckon girls that go out now, can look after themselves because if my mum locked me away until I was eighteen and I wasn't allowed out I would have been raped or anything. But now that I know the blokes around here, you've got to be careful. I've never been in a situation which I can't get out of and I'm only sixteen.
Janet: If you parents lock you away until you're around eighteen and then they let you out then you can't handle it, you don't know what you're in for.
IW: What do you mean by 'can't handle it' and 'you know how to look after yourself'? You mean there are situations you can get yourself into and...
Lucy: Some girls can't get out of it, you know. You just talk yourself out of it. Or you just walk off and you know how to handle it...kinda thing. But if mum locked me away, and then I got out at eighteen, I wouldn't know what the blokes are like.
IW: What's the difference between learning when you're sixteen and learning when you're eighteen. Won't you be just as vulnerable?
Lucy: When you're young, you've got more time to work it out. It's easier to know what they're like. I mean at eighteen I wouldn't be hanging around with those creeps.
Janet: It sounds stupid, starting young, but if you start going out when you're young and that and gradually go out more and more and more you get experienced with blokes and things like that and you know what you're in for. Whereas if you start at eighteen and you just go out at nightime, you don't know what you're in for.

If you've been held back, it's...it'll sound stupid to you but if it was me and I'd been held at home until I was eighteen, I'd say, 'Righty oh, I'm going to go out and rage'. And if you go out and rage, that's when you get yourself into trouble.

You see we know what's happening. If you've never had experiences with blokes before, and you go out, like you might go to some bar or something, and you sit there having a couple of drinks and a bloke will come up and say, 'Do you want to come out here and there with me?' And you say, 'Oh yeah, righty oh. Sounds good'. And next thing you know you're way out bush and he's saying something like, 'Fork it or walk it' and you don't know what the hell he's talking about.

. . .

Lucy: When I first went out, I used to go out and just be with my girlfriend. Now I've started meeting blokes and they used to introduce me to other blokes and then I'd get to know their personalities and meet other blokes and I'd know theirs and I'd know which one was bad and which one was good.

But at eighteen, you just say, 'Well in a couple of years I'm going to be twenty, I'm getting old so I may as well start living it up while I can'.

Janet: Like when you're young you hear about things like getting stuff slipped into drinks and things like that so you know, if you're going to go out, you watch your drink. I mean you don't stare at the glass, but you know just to check it and make sure no one's put anything in it.
Lucy: At eighteen you'd probably say, 'Oh it's just a drink, don't worry about it'.
Janet: Like there was a friend I used to know and she was just doing that and someone slipped something in her drink and she went for a really bad trip and she was really sick.

Throughout these passages Lucy and Janet draw a continual comparison with the imaginary locked-up 18-year-old who is less experienced than they are and who suffers for it. The 18-year-old is naive and easily conned. She has repressed impulses which, when released, only lead to disaster: 'And if you go out and rage, that's when you get yourself into trouble.' The locked-up 18-year-old is basically a very vulnerable person in the 'dangerous world' of adolescent social life.

The choice of 18 is revealing. Eighteen is the magical age, the age when Lucy and Janet officially become adults. In choosing an imaginary 18-year-old for their 'other', Lucy and Janet are voicing their resentment at being told to wait until they are 18 to be formally granted the maturity they already see themselves as possessing. The way they depict this 18-year-old is also revealing. All the characteristics of vulnerability which they project on to her are the same characteristics they believe they would be hampered by if they were to be locked up themselves: naivety, repressed urges, inexperience. It almost becomes a duty to be going out at sixteen.

The way Lucy and Janet present themselves in these passages reinforces this general impression. Both speak as if they are very experienced. Janet, for example, makes it sound as if she regularly goes to bars. She adds to this an almost patronising rejoinder, to some imaginary naive peer, about the need to avoid being obvious when you watch your drinks. She knows to keep an eye on her drink, but not to stare at it. Janet's overall depiction of herself involves creating this impression of an experienced, worldly woman, well able to cope with dealing with men and with nightlife.

In a way these passages contain the substance of a polemic with their absent parents. Lucy and Janet are arguing their case for greater freedom against their parents, but they are arguing it through me. This is why they present themselves in this particular way and give such weight to the impression of worldliness. But in the course of doing this, Janet and Lucy also open a window into another world, that of their peer group and the kinds of people and activities that happen there. This world is one where young women like Janet and Lucy must quickly learn a set of survival strategies in order to cope with an exploitative male environment. They are under no illusions about the dangers and the consequences of any lapses in one's survival strategies: 'And next thing you know you're way out bush and he's saying something like, "Fork it or walk it"...'

When Lucy mentions, several times, the 'blokes around here', she is alluding to this exploitative environment which forms a kind of background assumption for all her references to going out with men. For a more explicit account of what these men are like, Lucy offers the following episode:

> I went out with these blokes. They used to drink beer and that and they used to do things like that [treat sex as a challenge] and anyway, everytime they got one [sex with a woman], they used to put the tab of the can up on the wall. Anyway, I went to their place, I was with some girls—I always go with girls when I'm going to blokes places—and anyway, I said, 'What's that on the wall?' because there's all different bottle tops with guys names on top. And they said, 'Oh, that's how many we get, you know, in such a time'. And I felt real sick and I said, 'Look I'm going, are you coming or not girls?'
>
> So we took off and we never been back. We know they're just after one thing, and we're not a piece of shit you just shovel around when you want it.

Episodes like these quickly teach Lucy and Janet the need to develop their survival strategies. Already several such strategies are apparent.

Lucy has mentioned the need to get to know men's 'personalities' and the importance of meeting enough men so that one has more than just appearance to judge by. Lucy is concerned to develop the means to judge the 'good' from the 'bad'. These judgments become more sophisticated as a continuing relationship develops. There are 'tests' to gauge sincerity:

> *Lucy*: You have tests when you go out, don't you. You see if they treat you like a shit in front of their mates and that kind of thing. If they treat you like that, what the heck. [Makes a dismissive gesture]
> *Janet*: You get some blokes who'd be prepared, not to go out with

their mates in a group, but to take you out separately. Oh...how can you put it. You know how you see a big gang of blokes and a big gang of chicks and they'll all group up and go out together in pairs, you know, and they say, 'Oh look, I've got the best looking one' or something like that. But if he's a bloke who really likes you, he'll be prepared to stay clear of his mates when he takes you out.

And there is always the ultimate test:

> *Janet*: Just put it down to the test. If he asks for it [sex] I'll say no and if he keeps on coming back, you'll know he really likes you, but if he doesn't and he goes away calling you names, you know he's only after one thing.

For Janet and Lucy, 'going out' is basically an apprenticeship into adult social life. The vulnerability which results from being young and from venturing into a world which is fundamentally sexist means that 'passing the course' involves quickly learning a number of different strategies. Lucy and Janet learn to discriminate between men who are 'genuine' and those who are 'only after one thing'. They learn to discern the 'personality' beneath the veneer. It was also apparent in the earlier passages that they also learn to judge the degree of risk in different situations, to watch their drinks and not to go to men's places alone.

The enemy is not always obvious. As well as the blatantly exploitative males, there are the traitors within:

> *Janet*: You have other hassles as well. Of friends. There's some so-called friends, that are jealous of you, you two having a good relationship, and they will do anything to break it up. That's how I broke up with the bloke I was going with, the one I had a really good relationship with, because the kids started rumours about him and other chicks and me and other blokes, just to get us to split up cause they were jealous that they can't have that relationship. I mean it's not just the bloke and the chick. Sure they're 99 per cent of what's happening but there's also the people that are around you. They also have a great effect on the relationship.

By now it should be obvious that the sexual relationships in which these young people are involved are not simply personal relations but rather power relations. Sex is merely the currency in a larger exchange where the real issues are power and prestige. The struggles which emerge here branch out in many directions. There is the continual battle for maturity against parents. There are the power struggles with their peers, the exploitative men and the women of dubious loyalty.

The power struggles with the exploitative males are fundamentally one-sided and this is encapsulated in the 'good old double standard', the sexist ideology which endorses male promiscuity and vilifies similar female behaviour. For the men who Lucy and Janet know, sexual promiscuity within their peer network is a matter of great prestige, of being 'tough':

Janet: They think it's tough, they really do.
Lucy: And then they go and talk about it with their mates and that makes you really sick.

In Lucy's and Janet's eyes, their male acquaintances devalue sex to the point where it is only an extension of their egos. It has no emotional significance or personal meaning for them and only bears fruit in the bragging which takes place afterwards with their mates. This makes it difficult for these women to give to sex the meaning that they might want it to have in terms of affection and sharing. Here is how Debbie, another resident at the refuge, sums up this predicament:

Debbie: Like I really enjoy sex, I really do. But I just don't like pushy people, I don't like sneaky people. I just think everybody should be natural... Like men especially, there's heaps of peer group pressure, 'My mate had a good screw last night, so I'm going out to get one off some slut'. I think a guy just wants a screw so he can brag about it to his mates. Cause I've worked with so many men and I've just heard them bragging, bragging, bragging and bragging. Just makes me sick.

And they don't seem very natural at all. It doesn't mean anything to them. Like a guy has a screw with this chick he's just picked up. There's no meaning in it. Like sex is something that should have meaning and it should be beautiful. Not just sex, it should be beautiful, something really beautiful. And they're just abusing women, it's more abuse than anything. I don't think that's right at all.
IW: Should women be promiscuous like men?
Debbie: I don't think that's right. Women should have a bit more respect for themselves. Like if she likes sex, that's cool... but she shouldn't let her body be abused...

Debbie's final comments capture well the essence of the double standard. There is really no way that a woman can engage in sexual relations as freely as a man because, within the context of sexist social relations, that promiscuity amounts to being abused.

It is encapsulated in the label 'slut', a term of abuse which exactly mirrors the one-sided nature of the whole contest:

> *Janet*: Another thing that bugs me... you get used to blokes coming in and saying, 'Over the last week I've had this many chicks'. If a girl walked in and said, 'I managed to get it out of ten blokes over the last week', she would get the worst name out. They'd call her a slut. Like you can go around calling blokes sluts too, because most of them are.
> *Lucy*: But no one takes it that they are.
> *Janet*: It makes you really angry.

Ruth, one of the youth workers, notes with exasperation:

> It's a compliment for the boys to be called a slut. You know, it boosts their egos a little. Everyone says 'You're a slut' and they say, with a smile: 'Yeah, I know.' The boys here are so sexist, it's sick.

The obvious anger which Janet, Lucy and Debbie feel towards this hypocrisy testifies to their awareness of the basic injustice which this uneven power struggle involves. The contest has never been an even one; it is loaded against women from the start. The men usually monopolise the key resources, such as money and cars. Moreover, they possess most of the ideological weapons with which to reinforce that dominance.

This is particularly evident with regard to the ideological messages which women receive almost daily. Sexist ideology directs at young women two competing demands: they are encouraged to be sexually attractive yet they are also pressured into being sexually inactive. The message from their peers and from the media, from nearly every advertisement, from cars to milk, tells them to glamorise themselves as objects and to make themselves available to catch the male eye. Yet the messages of virginity that bombard them from parents and the ever-present danger of the label slut from their peers, enjoins them to deny the full expression of that sexuality.

The standard against which young women measure themselves, particularly the one created by the media, is constructed in such a way that only a tiny proportion of women ever achieve it. For those women without the slim figures, the silky hair, the unblemished skin, their happiness and sense of worth can be insidiously undermined by 'failure' in the glamour stakes. Here is how Maria, an 18-year-old volunteer worker at the refuge, experienced this process:

I know that at home they wanted me to do well at school and all the rest of it but still it was important that I was attractive, that I was slim and all those things and I took those things to the extreme. I wasn't happy with me, I could do a lot of things, but I was never happy with me, because I wasn't skinny and I starved myself to the point of being really sick and nearly dying just for all these things...

In the home is where I got all that original pressure. An Italian home: 'Here is my beautiful daughter who is now going to make coffee.' This thin sort of thing...

At school you could fall back on your academic success and if you had a good personality and people liked you, you could fall back on that too. But if you didn't succeed as a sex object, or sexually or whatever, you didn't have the important thing and you still fight with that now. That's still a big thing in my life. As much as I try and tell myself: 'This is not the important thing. Having human relations is important, having friends is good.' But it's not the only thing, it's still very much a part of me... I'm surrounded by it every day, by my mother who can't be happy because she hasn't got a man...

Young men too must come to terms with similar social pressures. They too must fashion an identity and salvage a sense of worth amid the range of competing conceptions of masculinity. They too search for models among their peers, their family and in the media. But for young women the process is fundamentally sexist because the models they are offered reduce them to objects which are deliberately fashioned for male consumption. The qualities which women are judged by, particularly physical appearance and acquiescence, are qualities which are valued either because they can be consumed by men or because they allow men dominance in any interactions.

Male dominance has traditionally relied on controlling women's fertility and sexuality. Modern contraception has increasingly removed male control in the first of these areas (though the current counterattack against abortion shows how tenuous that victory remains). But men are often still in control of women's sexuality, though with variations across class and culture. This male control is exercised in at least two ways. As the above discussion about objectification shows, men define what counts as 'attractive'. Male control of the media, particularly advertising, means that only a very limited definition of female sexual attractiveness receives widespread endorsement. Second, men control women's sexuality by enforcing sanctions which prescribe the degree of freedom women should be allowed in expressing their sexuality.

The label 'slut' is a graphic illustration of one of these sanctions. In essence 'slut' is a patriarchal code word meaning that a woman is only valuable as a sexual object and that object is one which must be kept pure for the exclusive use of a single male. Here is an account which one of the youth workers provided of a conversation he had with a 15-year-old resident:

> Jason has just come home from school and is telling me about the people there. He refers to one girl who is 'a bit of a slut'. Realising I don't approve of that word, he tries to justify his statement by saying, 'Well, she is making things bad for herself when she gets married'.
> *Stuart*: What do you mean?
> *Jason*: She'll be stretched. Spoiled for her husband.
> *Stuart*: Eh?
> *Jason*: You know. Her, um, vagina will be too stretched from all the screwing around.
> *Stuart*: You're saying that a girl who...
> *Jason*: Yeah, she gets sorta loose muscles.
> *Stuart*: But what about a woman with one partner who fucks with him a lot? Will she be...stretched?
> *Jason*: Aw no. It's only with a lot of different guys cause of all the different sizes of the cocks... [Indicates by showing me first a pencil, then his fist and forearm].
> *Stuart*: And what about giving birth, then?
> *Jason*: Oh that's OK. Cause it's sorta like your arse. It's alright for things to go out, but not the other way.
> *Stuart*: Well, what about a man who fucks a lot? Won't his cock get worn down or something?
> *Jason*: [laughs] Oh no! That's ridiculous!

In these comments it is clear that a double standard, which should be so obvious, becomes hidden by being submerged in a mythology of sexual ignorance. This playground mythology is not simply misguided, it is also political because it is used to justify a double standard of sexual morality. What is most revealing about this passage is the general sentiment that a women ruins herself physically for her future husband by being sexually active: 'She'll be stretched. Spoiled for her husband.'

An identical sentiment surfaces in the following comments from two young Greek women in an inner-city school:

Nia: If you go out a lot, you end up getting a bad name. Especially among the Greek people, that's how it is.
Angela: Yeah, some of the Greek people, they like talking about other people's daughters. Like they say, because she goes out, she might have a boyfriend, she likes flirting about, they call her these names.
IW: Does that act as a kinda control on you two when you want to do things, worrying about that?
Angela: I get angry because they say things like that. I go out with my brother and they make up all these names. They do.
Nia: They believe firstly, you've got to be a virgin after you get married and once you start going out and all that, they say you're not a virgin, even if you are. Like once you're flirting with guys, they think you're not a virgin. And that's what they pass around, that you're not a virgin.
Angela: Yeah, there's this lady I know, she talks about other chicks, other girls you know, but she doesn't look at her own daughter, while other people talk about her daughter, cause she's just as worse.
IW: But with the boys growing up...
Angela: Oh they don't get anything.
Nia: They don't say anything about the boys.
IW: Why is it so important for a girl to be a virgin when she gets married but not for a bloke?
Angela: OK the guy's got freedom but he also wants to respect his wife. He doesn't want to know that she's been around with every guy.
IW: But it mightn't be every guy, it might just be one or two. Why does that matter?
Nia: It does.
Angela: He wants to respect his wife. Like, just say they have an argument and he brings up the past or something, and that might get the girl, like if she hasn't done anything, he can't say anything about it.
IW: Is that right though, that a girl should be in that position of having to worry about that?
Angela: I don't know.
IW: Do you think it is necessary for you both to be virgins when you get married?
Angela: Yeah.
Nia: Yeah.
IW: Why?
Angela: Cause I think my husband will trust me more you know. He won't think, 'Oh look, she's been...you know'... Like if you're not a virgin and you do marry someone and that guy finds out, he might leave you, you know.

IW: What about if you tell him when you first meet him, or when you first get married?
Angela: He might leave you still then.
IW: Well is he worth having then? If that matters so much to him, if he doesn't value you for all the other things which...
Nia: It might not matter to him in most cases, but it does to his parents and his relatives.
Angela: Like most guys now, they say, 'Oh it doesn't really matter because no one's staying a virgin'. But still they might only be using you, you know, you don't know.
Nia: Maybe they just want that one thing out of you.
Angela: You don't know if you have sex with him whether he's going to leave you or not. He might leave you, then again, he might not.
Nia: Then if he does, then that reputation, you know, he might tell his friends.
Angela: And they usually do.
IW: Do you think there's a double standard there where blokes don't have the same problem, because all the things we're talking about are really only problems for girls? Do you think that's fair?
Nia: But you wouldn't expect a guy to be a virgin.
IW: But is that right though? You think you should be a virgin for your husband so he can trust you and not leave you, but you're not going to worry if he's not.
Angela: No. I wouldn't worry about it.
Nia: No.
IW: Why, that's not fair is it?
Nia: I don't know. I don't expect my husband to be a virgin.
Angela: None of the girls expect their husbands to be virgins.
[General laughter]
IW: But is it fair?
Angela: I've never really thought if it's fair or not.

The parallels here with the world of Lucy and Janet are many. These young women face the same predicament of attempting to determine when men are interested in them for an enduring relationship and when men are simply wanting casual sex. They too must face the expression of male egotism and the threat that presents to them: 'that reputation...he might tell his friends ...and they usually do.' In a strangely ironic way, the heavy emphasis on virginity is actually a form of protection for them. They realise that men have seized on the greater 'freedom' which the permissive society has offered women and have put this to their own use:

> Like most guys now, they say, 'Oh it doesn't really matter because no one's staying a virgin', but still they might be only using you, you know, you don't know.

Again the insight from Debbie fits in. Promiscuity within sexist social relations only amounts to abuse, not real liberation. So too, while virginity may be a trap whereby women are reserved for the exclusive use of one man, under conditions of sexist social relations, it is also a haven from exploitation by many men.

There are also ways in which the world of Nia and Angela is different from that of Lucy and Janet. The latter face their most formidable obstacles among their peer group, with parents more or less tucked away as nuisances in the background. For Angela and Nia however, parents are at the forefront of the battlefield. Parents and other relatives, indeed the local community as a whole, continually monitor the behaviour of Nia, Angela and their friends. The sanctions they most fear are levelled at them from that quarter: 'they like talking about other people's daughters...they make up all these names...' This also means that community standards, such as male promiscuity being acceptable, are also sanctioned from that quarter. So all the while the men are permitted, even encouraged, to be 'free', the torrent of messages about virginity and reputation engulf the young women.

The fundamental parallel between this passage and the one from Jason can now be seen. The Greek community through its patriarchal ideology defines these young women in terms of objects possessing particular qualities. Above all else they must be virgins, and any 'indiscretions' (whether real or only suspected) immediately pollute that object and render it worthless in the exchanges which make up the marriage market within the Greek community. Jason was also concerned about women being spoiled for their husbands. In his case it is a cruder version: it's not a question of reputation, trust or any other social characteristic, it's simply a question of being physically spoiled. Nevertheless, the perspective of both passages is identical: women owe it to their future husbands to safeguard their status as objects; they have absolutely no role as sexual beings in their own right.

Of course, in reality young women do assert their roles as

people in their own right, as autonomous sexual beings. They do continually make decisions and demand that their feelings be counted. The discussion about survival strategies earlier in this chapter highlighted this fact. Those strategies are basically concerned with learning to be an autonomous person in a minefield of exploitative males where the continual expectation is that women should only be objects. Because this expectation smothers so many areas—the peer group, the media, the school and the family—the struggle to remain an autonomous person is an unremitting one.

When a relationship develops with a young man, young women like Janet and Lucy are increasingly forced to make decisions, to be active in building their side of the relationship. But how does a young woman know how the relationship is developing? Where do the standards come from which allow assessments to be made? Again there is the media and the peer group, and not surprisingly, both are heavily infiltrated by sexist romantic ideology:

Janet: Even warped things like *Days of our Lives*, they have an effect on you... Like you might see on TV, a bloke and a chick getting on really well and going out to dinner in little quiet restaurants. To you it looks as if those two people were made for each other whereas in real life, you think to yourself, 'He's not taking me out to quiet dinners, you know, candlelight dinners'. You're saying you haven't got anything going...

It's the same with the magazines. They'll write up a story in the magazines. A lot of people read romances, I read romances, and they're all crap, the whole lot of them, none of them are true stories... you don't actually say to yourself, 'I read in the book that these two couples were doing this and that' but it's sorta there, in the back of your mind...

It's just the same as seeing a couple... they're doing all these things together, little things you notice from them. And then you have a relationship with a bloke, and you say, 'We're not doing this and we're not doing that' because those people are doing it and they're getting on really well. 'We're not doing it. We mustn't be made for each other.'

Clearly male dominance within the peer group is strongly endorsed by male dominance within the wider society. On the level of ideas, the media plays a crucial role, as the quote above illustrates. On the level of lived experience, the institutions which young people pass through are fundamental in shaping their aspirations. The next chapter will show how this is so for the family. As for the school, Dale Spender's work amply demonstrates how male control of knowledge and male dominance within classroom interactions are fundamental in restraining women's educational futures.[14]

The women in this chapter know this implicitly. The power struggle within the peer group transfers smoothly into the classroom:

> *Lucy*: I do woodwork at school and there's only two of us in the class, two girls. They're always putting us down cause we don't know how to use the wood and all the tools and because we don't know all the names of the tools and they crack jokes and everything like this. But we just said a couple of months before the end of last year, we said to ourselves, 'We'll show them what we're made of'. And we got higher marks than all the boys in the class so we were proud of that.
> *IW*: How did the boys react?
> *Lucy*: They don't say anything now. This year we've gone into woodwork and they don't say nothing now. We proved our little thing.

This passage shows clearly how the battle lines are drawn up. The men use knowledge as power: 'we don't know all the names of the tools and they crack jokes and everything.' The women respond by outdoing the men at their own game, by being better than them in the merit stakes.

In a way, the women win the battle but lose the war. Both Lucy and Janet, despite aspirations for non-traditional careers, have finally accepted that their futures lie in hairdressing and fashion design.[15] The reason for the backdown? Continuing gender harassment, both blatant and subtle:

> *Lucy*: When I first started third form, I wanted to be a panel beater and I went into it and I was really into that kind of thing, doing spray painting and sign writing. Cause the teachers used to say I was good at doing writing and I used to do it on scrap bits of paper and just sort of muck about and I went into it and that and I went down to the tech and then I found out there's only a couple of girls in it. And I felt really bad because you know there's about 30 in the class and I'd be the only bird in there. And this girl was talking to me and she said that it's really hard cause the blokes sorta putting you down so it's harder for a girl to get through than a bloke. She said it was hard but she made it. But I think that hairdressing's more my thing.
>
> *Janet*: I wanted to be a pilot at one stage and then, it was years ago,

just when they were going on about women pilots, and I thought, 'Stuff that, I'll be a hostess'.
IW: What made you change, the fact that it looked so hard to get in?
Janet: Yeah.
IW: You didn't want the hassles?
Janet: I didn't want all the hassles.

This gender harassment is extremely diverse and is located in many different areas. There is the blatant harassment from the men: 'you're trying to do it and be as equal as them and they're sorta putting you down!' There is simply the incredible weight of that ever-present knowledge that it will be an uphill battle to try and break out of the traditional areas. When one woman loses, she loses it for the rest. Even when one woman wins, the struggle involved can be enough to discourage the others:

> She said it was hard but she made it. But I think that hairdressing's more my thing.

and

> it was years ago, just when they was going on about women pilots, and I thought, 'Stuff that, I'll be a hostess'.

There are also the subtle pressures to conform, to be accepted within the peer group:

Lucy: I've always had B+s, usually. Never get a C. I always get B or B+. I've got some As but I've always been average and that's the way I like it. I can always get better or I can get worse.
Janet: The kid's say, 'She got straight As. She's a square, she's no good'.
Lucy: The guys we get around with, they're nice and that, but they're the same as us, we're always average. You know, that's the way I like to be. I wouldn't never like to get straight As. Like when I got a hundred out of a hundred for me test, I said I must have cheated. I even told the teacher and then I turned around and said I did. I didn't cheat but I wanted to get me scores down so I wouldn't get an A. That's what I did to meself.
IW: Do these grades really tell you anything about yourself?
[Silence]
Lucy: If you get a B or something, you're average. That means you're average in your personality and everything...

Devaluing oneself academically to gain social acceptance appears to be prevalent among many young women. Dale

Spender offers the following insights:

> ...when I interviewed fifteen-year-old girls at one London comprehensive, and asked them if they ever told the boys that they got high marks, or felt they were more capable, one girl summed it up for all when she said to me, 'What are you, miss? Stupid?'
>
> They all volunteered the information about the way they camouflaged positive performances...Most of them stated explicitly that they pretended they were dumb in the presence of boys who 'mattered' and expressed the sentiment that 'it doesn't pay for girls to be too bright'.
>
> This is consistent with findings in the United States where, as early as 1947 and 1949, studies indicated that female students pretended intellectual inferiority when talking to males...[16]

When women try to break out of this pattern, not only do they encounter hostility from men who feel threatened by a 'clever woman', but they also encounter resistance from 'gentlemen' who insist on 'helping'. After all, sexist ideology insists that women are not only passive, but dependent as well.

Fighting this ideology is a constant struggle. Here is how Eleanor, one of the only women at her university attempting to combine computer studies and law, must continually fight for her independence:

> When I first got here I'd go into the computer terminal room and try and figure out something and I didn't know anything about it but I'd sit there and I was determined I was gonna plod away until I'd worked it out for myself. And these blokes would lean over my shoulder and literally do everything for me and they wouldn't let me do it. They'd say, 'Look you've done that wrong. This is the way you do it'.
>
> I was really steaming because I didn't want to be shown and if I'd been a male they wouldn't have been trying to show me. They could just see me, this poor little helpless female not being able to do it because I'd just sit at the terminal swearing and so on. It was just I wanted to do it by myself and I think finally I gave most of them that message. But that was something that really infuriated me.

If personal relations are power relations and if young women implicitly understand this, what prevents a more concerted attack on the unequal nature of those power relations?

One answer is that the obvious physical dominance of men is cemented into most of the structures these women move through. There is the fear of rape, ever present in the night: 'I ran away in the nightime and I was scared and I thought I might get raped.'

There is the male monopoly over mobility: the men own all the cars and set the terms for offering transport. The panel van as *the* adolescent car typifies this. But the unequal power relations are also embedded in women's environments in more subtle ways. There is an emotional investment in being a successful object for others, an investment which devalues the areas where one exists as an autonomous person. As Maria put it:

> At school you could fall back on your academic success... but if you didn't succeed as a sex object... you didn't have the important thing and you still fight with that now.

In negotiating this unequal power struggle, a structural perspective would be an obvious asset. To be able to transcend the individual instance of things and realise that what is happening is part of a larger process, one that involves *all* men and *all* women, would enable young women to evolve strategies which go to the heart of the power struggle. It is at this very juncture that the ideology of individualism intrudes. It was apparent earlier in this chapter that Lucy found it important to learn to discriminate between the good and the bad men whom she met. While on one level this was an obvious asset in dealing with immediate male exploitation, on another level it still leaves her locked into a particular pattern of domination by men. Here is how Lucy described breaking up with her first boyfriend:

> He treated me like a shit. First of all he didn't. He's one of those sorta devil types. He didn't for about seven months. He was real quiet for about seven months and then all of a sudden he started hitting me because I didn't do what he wanted me to do.
>
> For seven months I was wrapped in him and then when he started hitting me I just took it and everyone thought I was bloody stupid. Then all of my friends just put this will power into me. They made me realise that he's just a big shit. He's no good for me. I was upset for a couple of days and things like that. Now I think back and say, 'How the hell did I go with him'.

On a later visit to the refuge I asked about Lucy and her boyfriend and learnt that they were back together again. On my next visit, the situation had changed yet again:

> *IW*:   In the conversation with Lucy, she was saying that she had finally come to see the light, that he was no good and the next time I came around here, I think you mentioned to me that she had gone back to him.

Ruth: Well she finally did see the light and she stayed away but then she was going out with other guys who were just as bad.
IW: So it wasn't a real break from that?
Ruth: A break from him. It was a break from that particular one. She's gone on to others of the same.
Stuart: As you've probably noticed yourself, a lot of their talk, their feelings about what they've done, is individualised. It's this particular boy is no good, so I'll find another one but he may have exactly the same macho type of characteristics but it's another one so we've got a chance with him.

The only real chance, for Lucy and her peers, lies not with any one particular male, but with a new set of social relations in which maleness is no longer constructed in exploitative and sexist ways.

5
'The way it's always been'

Janet: I was eleven when I first tried to commit suicide. I got an old chaff sack, and I tied rocks to the bottom of it...and I put it over the top of me, like you set a glass upside down on the table. And I jumped in, and of course the rocks pulled me down.
IW: Into the water?
Janet: Yeah. This was when we were still at the horsestud where I'd been given a horse... And he really meant a lot to me. He meant more to me than my family did. No one else could ride him, he was just a one-person horse. I looked to him for attention... I got more attention from him than I did from my parents and it was then that I said, 'Stuff, I'll be leaving Boxer behind'. So I climbed...I don't know how I got out, but I just sorta crawled out and swam up to the top.
IW: What made you do it?
Lucy: I suppose you felt like you couldn't get anywhere.
Janet: Yeah, that's exactly what I felt like. That was when I first felt I wasn't being treated like a human being. I felt like a can on the production line. I didn't feel like a person. I just felt like I was there and I wasn't serving any purpose.

Like Lucy, Janet also smokes continually as she talks. She is recounting her family background, offering reasons for why she is here, today, living in a youth refuge. The immediate reasons for moving out of home were fights with her mother about how much freedom she should have. But the tensions in her family life go back many more years before that.

Janet spent the first part of her secondary schooling in a boarding school, an experience she would sooner forget. Yet living back at home with her family was equally depressing. There was a continuing rivalry with her brother:

My brother, he dropped out of school when he was in third form and I kept through to the end of fourth form. I thought, that's one thing

I've got against him. That's one I've got up on him. People lick their fingers and stick it up on the board, that's what I did.

And then I thought about it and said, 'He's a dole bludger, living off mum. You know, like a leech. He's sucking up to mum and living off her, like a leech does'. That's how I always picture my brother, like a leech.

Another thing I've conquered, I've kept on up to fourth year and I've been able to stand on my own two feet. That's one thing he can't do...I think that's a reason I don't like the dole, cause he's on it.

Of all the family relationships though, it was the hypocrisy and exploitation by her father that most offended her:

I was getting really fed up with my father.... He used to always sorta, put me on display. I was the eldest daughter...I was working for him in the holidays, just in the office, answering phones, typing out letters and stuff like that. He sells cars, Mercedes, and he'd bring in all the diplomats, and he'd say, 'This is my daughter'. And it must have been something about blond hair, there must be something special about kids having blond hair. Cause he used to always comment on my hair, 'Keep it long. Keep it long'. Make sure I kept going out in the sun so that it'll get blonder and blonder. All sorts of stuff like that. He used to bring people in and say, 'This is my long blond-haired daughter'. It really used to bug me. It got to the stage where I wanted to dye my hair black. And that's when I start having it cut...

The thing that bugged me was when I was home he used to treat me like I was, excuse the expression, a shit... It seemed to me he used to pick on me at home. I always had to be neat and perfect. He used to treat me really badly at home. And then he used to take me out and he'd show me off to all the other people...and when you got home it was so completely different... He was all mixed up because one minute he's saying, 'This is my daughter' and the next minute he's saying, 'You're too young'. They won't let you out. One minute they're saying, 'Why don't you go out with such and such a person's son?' Next minute they're saying you can't go out with that bloke. Like it was all for the business.

Janet's comments offer a vivid insight into how male control of female sexuality occurs in terms of ageism. In being exploited as an object by her father, Janet's feelings as a person are completely neglected. Patriarchal family life is invariably oriented towards the economic and social position of the father−husband. In the case of Janet's family, her personal happiness is sacrificed to the needs of the business. She is unhappy at home but she is forced to fit the veneer of the 'businessman's happy family' on parade to the outside world. The hypocrisy of this whole charade angers her deeply. It angers her that she is recognised as sexually mature when it suits her father—'This is my daughter'—and then denied this when it's in her own interests: 'You're too young'.

After her parents divorced, Janet lived with her mother, but the conflicts over social freedom worsened and eventually she found herself staying at the refuge. Janet is impressed by the transition from a situation of dependency within her family to the independence which communal living offers:

> I like looking after myself, I enjoy it. Cause then if I make any mistakes, I blame it on myself and I'll know not to do it again. Whereas if I was at home and I made a mistake, I'd blame it on everyone at home and not me and I keep on making the mistake. But here I'm independent.
>   Like it's weird. When I was at home, I used to go out a lot, and if I couldn't go out I used to fight with my mum. Whereas while I've been here I've hardly gone out at all...
>   Another thing I like is I enjoy cleaning the place up. I mean, it may not seem like it. I may have a negative attitude, but I enjoy it. I don't like doing dishes and I don't like cleaning up the house but I'm enjoying the responsibility... Here I get treated more as an adult, more like a person.

However, for Janet communal living is only a reluctant alternative to the 'traditional' family and she admits later that she would prefer to be back with her family if things could be 'fixed up'. Nevertheless, her unhappiness has made her seriously question the place of marriage in her own future:

Janet: I've got to the stage where my parents as models don't have any effect on me. Because I say to myself, 'Oh, they've done this and that together, and they've been like this and she's done this and he's done that'. And then I say to myself, 'And they ended up with a divorce'. So I'll either ignore it completely or I'll say, 'I won't do that'. And then again, that might cause problems because that might not have been the reason why they had the divorce.
IW: Has it put you off marriage?
Janet: To you it may not sound like I've got any problems, but to me I've got problems and I'll say to myself, 'I don't want to have kids cause I don't want to them to go through what I've been through'. I say to myself now, 'I wanna have kids'. But I say to myself, 'I'm not going to have kids and I'm not going to get married'. I wanna meet the right bloke, settle down and get married and have kids, and go out and get a job and stuff like that. And eventually become a

grandmother. That's what I really want deep down inside, but
then...like I've got two people inside me. Like one person's saying
that and the other person's saying, 'Oh you think of what the hell
you've been through and then about your parents' marriage'. Like one
person's saying you want it and the next person saying, 'No way!'

This is the future Janet is speculating about. She seems to be ambivalent about what she really wants. Her parents' divorce and her own unhappy home life have discredited marriage and family life. Yet the cultural conditioning which equates happiness with family life runs very deep and climaxes in the phrase, 'and eventually become a grandmother'.

Despite her guarded reflections about the future, the considerable strength of Janet's emotional investment in 'traditional' family life is quite apparent in her comments about jealousy:

> It's only because I'm jealous that I haven't got that relationship with my parents. I've worked that out. I've sat down and thought about it.
> Like if I see a kid getting on really well with her parents, I get really jealous, I really do. It's what I really want but I know I can't have it. I know, my family, the relationship will never get back to how it was. And when I see someone my age getting on really well with her parents, I get really jealous, and I say to myself, 'There has to be something wrong with that family'. That's what I say to myself, sorta, so I wouldn't feel bad about it.

It comes as no surprise when I next return to the refuge to find Janet no longer resident. She and Lucy have returned home after new terms for their family relationships were negotiated. Lucy now boards in a caravan in her parents' backyard, an arrangement which allows her greater personal freedom while still maintaining the family unit intact. Janet found a job, and with her new economic independence, she was prepared to return to live with her mother.

This time I begin a conversation with Marg, the 16-year-old woman whom we met briefly in chapter 1. Marg grew up in a large Catholic family. Her father was a truck driver and prone to violence when drunk. Her mother spent most of her time arbitrating family conflict. For Marg, the hardest part of family life was coping with jealousy:

> *Marg*: I was the baby of the family for eight years and I'll admit it, I was pretty spoilt when I was the baby. And then mum fell pregnant with Tanya and I hated her, I really hated her. When she was born I'd

pinch her, I'd pinch her when mum wasn't looking and I really hated her and when she was starting to walk I'd push her over all the time. I just hated her cause, like everyone loves a new baby, and I was pushed out. But it's just the last couple of years that I've started to get used to it. And now Tanya and I are so close it's not funny.

Marg's adolescence was also marked by gender harassment by her elder brothers:

One time when I was really insulted... I was really embarrassed about being a girl. I just wanted to be a boy... I really hated it, the first time I got my periods right, and my sister, she was a real bitch at that stage. She was pregnant, and you know what women are like when they're pregnant. Anyway, she told my brothers and that really embarrassed me. They were saying, 'Oh she's a big mature woman now' and everything. And I really hated being a girl then. I just hated it so much...

For a couple of months I hated it, like I'd get hell. I thought it was so mean. Like I've never seen anyone act like that towards a girl and at that stage I just wanted to be a boy.

Her sister was pregnant and unmarried and this was a major family crisis during Marg's early adolescence. As a consequence, Marg finds tighter restrictions placed on her own social freedom. But the example of her sister shows Marg exactly what it is her parents most fear:

Marg: Do you know what they're worried about? Shame and pride. You know, like if I fell pregnant they wouldn't be able to handle the shame of it. Like they went through it with my big sister and they were just so shamed.

Marg does in fact develop a close relationship with a young man, Peter. Despite the developing trust, Marg faces all the same doubts which the women in chapter 4 discussed:

Marg: Like when me and Peter first had sex, I didn't know whether he was going to go and tell all his mates or see...
IW; Didn't you know him very well?
Marg: Yeah, I'd been going with him for five months... but still, guys are guys and they brag about sex and that.
   That's when I thought that people would think I was cheap, I didn't care what happened between me and Peter. It was what my name was going to be cause I hate to think people think I'm a mean thing and things like that.

The relationship also develops the same sexist role stereotyping which chapter 4 illustrated:

> Like I still have hassles saying, 'Oh Peter, are we going out tonight?' Like I can't really do it. I have to wait for him to say it.

This relationship coincides with Marg's religion becoming central for her again. This has happened through joining a charismatic sect within her church. Marg manages, however, to resolve the potential conflict between sex and religion:

> *Marg*: Like me and Peter having sex right? And that's against my religion, right? But I'm not feeling it's wrong because, like... Oh I can't explain it. Me and Peter are... As the priest said, 'If you really love the person and you know that it's not wrong in yourself, you know that it's not wrong, then it's not wrong'. Nothing's wrong that you don't think's wrong in yourself and you really know deep down inside that it's not wrong. If you have a touch of something that's saying it is wrong, just a little touch, then there's got to be something wrong.
> *IW*: Did you feel any guilt after the first time?
> *Marg*: Yeah, at first I did, because like, I think every girl does the first time.
> *IW*: So isn't that what you're talking about?
> *Marg*: I didn't feel guilt against my religion, I felt guilt against me.
> *IW*: Yeah, but that's what you're talking about isn't it, that if you get the slightest hint that it may be wrong...
> *Marg*: No. I felt guilt that I was cheap, see, that's what I felt guilt about. But I never felt...
> *IW*: That you were doing wrong?
> *Marg*: Yeah.

Marg has interpreted her priest's advice as approval for her sexual activity, even though it is explicitly forbidden by her church. This resolution of the problem takes place as a kind of trade-off: Marg ignores this particular teaching, because it is at variance with her immediate needs, and in return she accepts other, even more draconian teachings of her church. She refuses to use contraceptives and she is prepared to accept the birth of an unwanted child rather than seek an abortion.

'Even if the unwanted child is due to rape?' I query. Marg pauses and frowns. She does not pursue the issue of abortion but turns to consider the question of rape:

Marg: Rape is something I have to live with but there's nothing I can do about it and there's nothing anybody can. There's nothing rallies can do about it, women's lib or anything can do about people who are raping people because they can't help sick people, you know what I mean. They're still gonna be...
IW: You think people who rape are sick people?
Marg: Yeah, they're animals. And they are...like if they wanted to have a good time, they could go to a pro's place or something. But like if they like that for kicks, they must be animals.
IW: You don't think some men do it to keep women in their place? It's not that they want the kicks, it's just that they want to stay on top?
Marg: Yeah, but they're animals doing that, aren't they? They're still animals. Trying to prove that they're great. But you see there's nothing us women can do about it except stick together in it because, like there's always been rapes and there always will be and there's nothing anyone can do about it.
IW: And you just think it's sick people? You don't think it's every man is potentially likely to do that?
Marg: Well, I've known Peter's tried to rape me once. Like he realised what he was doing once he got too far cause like...
IW: Who's this, sorry?
Marg: My boyfriend. Like I wasn't in the mood and like he really was and I just kept on, 'No, leave me alone'. And like he got me down on the bed but he realised what he was doing before he done it.
IW: Doesn't that point to what I'm saying that everyone could potentially do that and it's not just sick people?
Marg: Yeah, but you see, in the way that Peter done it, I could have led him on, you see, or...
IW: Did you? Did you give him any encouragements?
Marg: No, not really. Like we were just sitting on the couch and watching TV. I think a guy can lead himself on.
IW: But what you're saying backs up what I'm saying, doesn't it?
Marg: A guy that goes out and rapes women after women after women, there has to be something wrong with them.
IW: Yeah. OK I agree with you. But what about all the rapes that take place among people that know each other? Cause a lot do. A lot of women get raped in their own home by people they think they know.
Marg: Yeah. Well I say they'd have to be sick too. Unless the man was led on.
IW: But if it's like Peter and they lead themselves on?
Marg: Oh well, he stopped before he was doing something wrong. He probably was sick at that stage too. I don't know, I just reckon that any man that was caught raping anyone should be castrated and that's the way I feel.

In this passage Marg is trying to explain her own personal experiences with an intellectual framework which continually leads to conservative conclusions. Despite her obvious loathing for male violence, Marg has nevertheless accepted a male definition of the problem: 'Rapists are sick people.' This makes the whole question of rape a personal problem, not a social one, and the focus on individual 'pathologies' obscures the way rape exists as a power relationship of men over women. The kind of defeatism which this individualistic diagnosis produces is very apparent in Marg's response. It's all a question of learning to 'live with it' because 'there's always been rapes and there always will be and there's nothing anyone can do about it'.

Marg's explanation starts to break down, however, when she brings her own experience with Peter into the discussion. There is now a radical disjuncture between her intellectual position and her lived experience. She attempts to patch this up with more sexist myths: 'Men who rape are led on by the women'. This doesn't last long, however, because Marg knows that she definitely did not lead Peter on. Intellectually Marg is left floundering. The patriarchal world view which constantly personalises social power relationships between women and men proves a major impediment in trying to understand the nature of her own experiences. Marg finally pulls out of this predicament by abandoning debate and retreating into her anger: 'I don't know, I just reckon that any man that was caught raping anyone should be castrated and that's the way I feel'.

Many churches and various anti-feminist groups have concentrated much of their attention on 'defending the family', which really means restricting women's economic and social roles to motherhood and domestic labour. When Marg outlines the ideal of family life which she wants in the future, these injunctions about women's role are never far away:

> *Marg*: I reckon that when you're married and you've got a family, a woman's place is at home in the house, looking after her children.
> *IW*: Why?
> *Marg*: I don't know, that's just the way I feel. That's the way it's always been and that's the way I think it should stay. And the man, they think they're big men, you know, and they're so great. I reckon, well, they should support the family. And that's just the way I feel.
> *IW*: But doesn't that mean that a man has all the contacts and gets out and that the woman is condemned to a do all the boring, dull housework.

Marg: Housework isn't boring and dull and like a woman gets out doing things. I love shopping. Like they do go shopping and they can go out. Like when their hubby comes home I reckon it's good the way a woman cooks the meal for him and I reckon it's good going out on family outings and things like that. Going out in the middle of the bush nowhere and just having a barbie. I reckon that's the way families should be.

IW: But you don't think that's unequal, that the woman's not getting as good a life as the man?

Marg: But she's not getting a different life than the man, like the man's working, same as the woman's working, except the man's working outside with people. And a man hates the work half the time. And like I think it's fair enough for the man to have, say, two beers on the way home from work if he wants to.

IW: Even if a man hates the job he's doing, he's meeting lots of people, he's getting money. The wife stays at home, doesn't meet anyone really and doesn't get paid.

Heather: She can go out with friends and that.

Marg: Yeah. No but you see like when I'm married I'll still have the friends I've got now and like they'll probably be married with kids and like when the kids are at school or even if the kids are in prams, like I could meet up with my friends and we could go shopping. Or we can take the kids to the park or if it's summer we can take them to the pool. There's just so much you can do.

IW: But you won't get paid for working at home. You won't have your own money. Don't you think that's unfair?

Marg: No, but you see the man brings the money home, right? And he should give the woman enough money to buy the groceries and say, enough money to do what she wants for her own personal self. Do you understand what I mean?

IW: You'd be happy with that situation?

Marg: Yeah.

IW: But there's a lot of women who aren't. Why do you think that is?

Marg: I don't know. They might be selfish. I'd say they're selfish.

IW: In what way?

Marg: Well, it's selfish for the children for a start.

IW: You don't think the husband can bring up the children?

Marg: No. If the woman had the kid. I mean the baby...

IW: But the husband had his bit to do in that?

Marg: Yeah, but not as much as the woman's. Like we had to put up with it for nine months. We had to go through all the agony at the end, didn't we?

IW: Yeah. Right.

Marg: And then we had to go through changing all the shitty nappies and that... I mean, if the woman doesn't want to be home

and if she wants her own life out with her own friends and wants to work and doesn't want to have anything to do with the home, I think that's selfish.
IW: In a way, that's what the husband's life is all about. He is being selfish, isn't he?
Marg: No.
IW: He's not doing his bit.
Marg: He is. He's bringing money into the house, right? And he's coming home and like the kids are always looking forward to their daddy to come home cause they've had their mummy all day, right? I know, I can't... Can you understand what I mean?
IW: Yeah. I can understand exactly what you're saying. I'm just wondering why you see it that way. Like the wife could go out to work and bring in the money. The husband could be at home bringing up the kids. It's exactly the same situation, isn't it? What's wrong with that?
Marg: I don't know. It's just the way I see it. I can't explain it, it's just the way I see it.

Conservative ideologies entrench themselves in people's thinking because they naturalise—and thus eternalise—social practices and institutions. It is common to hear, as a defence of some status quo, those numerous clichés which celebrate naturalness: 'it's only natural that...' 'you can't change human nature', and so on. These easily slide into 'that's the way it's always been (and will always be)'.

This has happened with the patriarchal form of the nuclear family. Marg begins her conversation with the phrase: 'That's the way its been and that's the way I think it should stay.' The rest of her comments stay within this avenue: it's natural for women to stay home, for men to go out to work. It's natural for women to be mothers and they're being selfish if they try to avoid this 'biological destiny'.

For many women, part of the trade-off for independence and worth as a person is the elevation of the domains of home management and motherhood since these are, in many cases, the only domains recognised as their own. Anywhere else they are seen as interlopers. Here is how Sandy, who spoke in chapter 1, speculates about her future married life:

> If I get engaged or anything I wouldn't mind at all settling down cause I think if I had a house and I was able to decorate it myself and everything... I would enjoy cleaning it and looking after it and also I think if I had a family I'd enjoy looking after them and making sure

everything's done and caring for them and all that kind of thing. I just think it's part of the role of living. You have to do it. Someone has to do it.

A similar trade-off is at work in Marg's picture of married life. Her whole conversation here amounts to an exploration of her family ideal, particularly the happiness it should offer. There are the family outings, like 'the barbie', and there is the mother going shopping with her girlfriends and taking the kids to the pool or the park. There is the 'good hubbie' having a couple of beers but then coming straight home to his expectant kids. These elements of family life are what Marg is really after and she is obliged, because of the way that conservative ideologies naturalise social institutions, to accept the current means for attaining this ideal, namely, the patriarchal form of the nuclear family. This then involves Marg accepting another 'natural' institution, the gender role of housewife where there is no prospect of gender equality. The argument about 'selfishness' swamps any possibilities of such equality. Conservative ideologies retain their dominance by screening out alternatives, by naturalising traditional institutions and making it seem that people's aspirations can only be fulfilled within a narrow range of options.

This is what happens with Marg. In real life, Marg's own family situation has been a very unhappy one. Her father regularly came home drunk. Her sister became pregnant at an early age. Her brothers were unemployed. Parental discipline was enforced through violence. This pattern of family life has not, however, discredited the patriarchal form of the nuclear family as an institution. It's simply the case that *her* family was a crummy one. Instead of seeking alternatives to the family in its patriarchal form, Marg accepts it as natural and proceeds to idealise its elements. She builds this ideal out of the ashes of her own sad experiences—parental violence, for example:

> Like with my parents they bash first and then they scream, you know. Instead, I reckon it should be talking, not screaming, you know, talking it out. And then if the kid needs a bash, give it a clip around the ear or something, not a bash, you know.

Similarly, Marg's idealised husband will only have two beers on the way home, an obvious rejoinder to her father's habitual drunkenness.

The issues raised in this chapter are not confined to families in conflict. As much feminist fiction shows, one of the central issues surrounding the patriarchal form of the nuclear family is the limited role of 'other' ascribed to women when they labour as 'housewives'. For example, in her remarkable novel *Gaining Ground*, Canadian writer Joan Barfoot recounts the story of a middle-aged woman, Abra, who suddenly leaves her husband and two young children. She exchanges a secure family life for a precarious solitude in a small remote cabin. As the story unfolds, the reader gains a vivid insight into how Abra's life, as a mother and a wife, is one lived entirely through and for others. Her identity as a person in her own right is constantly eclipsed by her domestic role as the 'other' for her husband and her children.

By the time Abra's family find her and try to reclaim her, the reader has a profound understanding of how crippled Abra's autonomy would be were she to return to those domestic roles. When her husband confronts her and tries to persuade her to return, he offers to procure psychiatric help. He is concerned that Abra should not face *her* 'problem' all alone and attributes her earlier departure to this neglect.

Abra's husband is kind and generous, a faultless 'family man'. Her young children are similarly virtuous. The remarkable achievement of Barfoot's novel is that she depicts Abra's deep unhappiness as the product of the *structure* of the patriarchal form of the nuclear family as an institution. Because the people involved are exemplary personalities, the reader is steered clear of blaming unhappiness on the actions or characteristics of individuals.

Joan Barfoot's novel eloquently explores the same themes which Janet's and Marg's reflections dwell upon. Taken together, they offer a fruitful understanding of how the twin pillars of patriarchal ideology—naturalism and individualism—serve to sustain a form of family life inherently based upon the oppression of women and children. The task of building viable alternatives to the patriarchal form of the nuclear family requires, as its groundwork, the demolition of those twin pillars.

6
Worlds apart

Debbie: This guy picked me up yesterday, as a matter of fact. Took me up in the bush... He offered me lots and lots of money and I told him to get fucked and he didn't like that very much. He grabbed at me and everything so I punched him. Punched him in the belly and got out of the car and waved down this ranger. 'Hey take me home.' And they did.
Steve: Did you know he was taking you there?
Debbie: Had a fair idea. Kept saying, 'Let me out. Let me out you fucking wog. Let me out'. I wanted to hit him in the knackers but he was sitting down, so I just went Whoof, and winded him and got out quickly and threatened to chuck rocks at him.
IW: Why did he act like that?
Debbie: He was a horny old bugger. That's what he was... He offered me money. Like it wasn't, like I don't think he would have, he would've raped me if I would've let him. Two hundred dollars for five minutes. I thought about it, the stupid thing was. An easy 200. Fuck, I wouldn't do it for $1000. Err, he smelt like garlic, made me sick... He was nice about it... He offered me ten dollars to begin with... He pulled out all these bills... I thought about it yesterday and I'll never hitch again, but today I hitched.
Claudia: I can't think of anything more revolting. Five minutes with this horrible man. Yuk.
Debbie: My sister does it all the time. Old men come into the place where she works. Oh yuk I couldn't do it. Doesn't matter how many bongs I get or I was offered. 'I'll give 200 bongs.' I'd say 'No'.

Debbie, Claudia, Stuart and myself are sitting a circle on the floor of the youth refuge. Debbie, who spoke briefly in chapter 4 is fifteen years old and a resident at the refuge. Claudia, who appeared briefly in chapter 3, is eighteen and works at the refuge as a part-time volunteer. Stuart, who also featured in chapter 4, is one of the full-time workers at the refuge.

Amid the coffee cups and cigarette butts, the conversation touches on many topics but settles for a while on the issue of sexual violence. Debbie had just come in from hitching a lift from town and I asked her if she thought that it was a safe thing to do. Of course it's safe, she replied, provided that you're not dressed like 'an easy lay'. Then, in the very next breath, Debbie launched into recounting the incident above.

Debbie's narrative touched off a memory in Claudia, an incident many months old but still fresh in its impact:

Claudia: One time I was in a parking lot with my friend walking back to the car and we were holding hands. And between us and the car were these men and women who all knew each other. But the men were getting really heavy with this particular girl and they were sort of simulating a rape. And it was getting really frightening because she was screaming and not enjoying it at all. And they were holding her and one man sort of groping at her and being really violent.

And it was really scary and we were very scared because they saw us and we looked like lesbians and all this sort of stuff. And as we came closer one started coming up, and you know, holding us and 'Give us a kiss' and all this. We were really terrified and broke free and jumped in the car and zoomed away. And that was about, oh, 12.30 or 1.00.

And when I told my parents about it, mum was silent and nodding, which means she understood what it was like... When we talked to dad, he started putting the blame on me and saying, 'You were out very late. You were in a parking lot alone. You shouldn't have been there'. He wasn't letting men off for doing it but he was saying I shouldn't have been there. It was my responsibility not to be in situations like that. And mum and I really cracked. We just said, 'No, wrong, wrong, wrong. I should have the right to be on the street when I want to be on the street et cetera...'

These two passages are both very similar and yet very different. On the one hand they starkly expose the real problems for young women of male sexual violence. On the other hand, they illustrate two entirely different responses to that problem, responses determined by two different life situations and two different levels of critical understanding.

Before looking at these life situations it is worth comparing the two passages more closely, looking at the different levels of understanding which each woman brings to bear upon her experiences.

It is obvious that each passage possesses a distinctive structure. Claudia's narrative is well developed in its chronological sequencing, its level of description and its inclusion of analysis.

By contrast, Debbie offers us only the barest outline at first, and rather than a chronological unfolding she repeats the episode a number of times, adding more details with each retelling. With Debbie, these details are added as a result of external questioning. For Claudia the analysis is built into the narrative and does not require the same external prompting.

Both women reflect upon their experiences, but they do it in different ways. Debbie and Claudia each possess different conceptual 'tools' with which to order their thinking, and the different structures in their narratives bear this out. Claudia analyses sexism and male motivations as she proceeds with her narrative. They are built into it as part of its logical unfolding: 'they were sort of simulating a rape' and 'we were very scared because they saw us and we looked like lesbians'. With Debbie, the analysis comes more slowly. Her understanding is formulated as she expounds her narrative: 'Like it wasn't, like I don't think he would have, he would've raped me if I would've let him.'

Claudia's conceptual tools are the legacy of twelve years of favourable educational experiences. Debbie stopped attending school at fourteen, and its legacy is mainly a set of bad memories. Claudia has also had fruitful contact with feminism and this becomes apparent in her narrative. Claudia perceives that what is happening in the street and what is happening at home with her father are both linked by the underlying patriarchal structure of unequal power relations between men and women. She is able to see how it generates violence in the streets and a chasm in understanding in the home.

In the narration of that violence, Claudia is not concerned with the individual inclinations of the men: they remain anonymous in terms of personal characteristics. They are merely the puppets for certain kinds of behaviour, behaviour which is defined as *male*. Even the moment of horror, when they were approached, is not described in terms of the characteristics of the men involved but rather in terms of the kind of situation of sexist intimidation in which they found themselves. The wording clearly implies that this situation was one commonly understood as a particular kind of male violence: 'You know, holding us and "Give us a kiss" and all this.'

The chasm in understanding which occurs at home divides along gender lines. The empathy between mother and daughter is based on sharing that common environment of male violence which, even when not overtly expressed, lies behind all the impositions and restrictions which curtail women's autonomy. It is these very restrictions which the father, as yet another male in this patriarchal power arrangement, attempts to defend: 'You shouldn't have been there.' Interestingly, the father's justification is not one which betrays the operation of this fundamentally unequal power relation but instead is couched in terms of parental concern.

Claudia herself rejects this. She does not reply within these terms of parental concern by saying, 'I can look after myself', as some daughters might argue. Rather, she replies by confronting the whole question of the unequal power relations between men and women: 'No, wrong, wrong, wrong. I should have the *right* to be on the street.'

Debbie, by contrast, offers an analysis which bears all the features of individualism. In this episode of being abducted, the violence which Debbie encounters derives, according to her, from the characteristics of the person: 'you fucking wog', 'a horny old bugger', and so on. The characteristics are, moreover, provided by racist and ageist ideologies.

These different responses, these different conceptual tools and ideologies, are the product of two very different life histories. According to Debbie, her parents grew up under extreme conditions of deprivation. Her father had no mother for most of his childhood and he was just 'dragged around in a cart' for most of his early years. As for her mother:

> My mother's father was very cruel to her, very cruel. He wouldn't let her go to school and he had her chopping wood, cooking and cleaning. Just doing everything all at once. And she brings that up when we're arguing, 'When I was younger, my father...'
> 'You might have deserved that,' I say, just to be cruel.

Debbie herself grew up in a family characterised by endemic domestic conflict. Her mother left home and, as in most patriarchal families, Debbie's educational future was sacrificed to the family's needs as she took on the domestic responsibilities of her departed mother. The bitterness engendered by this episode surfaces intermittently, particularly in fights with her mother:

> I always bring up something with my mum when we have a fight. 'You had an affair behind dad's back! You had an affair!' And that's like being burnt, but I have to bring it up. It's just to hurt her.

'You left me!' That's another thing I bring up. Like there's nothing wrong with a mother leaving her children, there's nothing wrong with it at all. She doesn't feel guilty until it's brought up and you pick at the bad points in it. There's really none but you make bad ones up.

I say, 'You left me. You left me with a heap of responsibilities that belong to you'. Like the poor woman was ready for a mental breakdown and here I just bring up all these things just to get at her. I can't forgive mum for just taking off. I can't forgive mum for having an affair. But I have forgiven, but I haven't.

I have to bring that up, just to hurt her, to score one. 'Listen mum, I'm going to hurt you...' My mum's always OD-ing and she's just so emotionally disturbed when we get into our arguments and she just freaks out. Like I've had her OD-ing. I've had her that way she ODed because I've just hurt her so much. And I've explained to her afterwards that I don't mean what I say, it just comes out.

Debbie lost little by leaving school early. As a working-class female in a schooling system geared towards middle-class males, Debbie's educational prospects were minimal to begin with. When she recalls her school days, it is to judge them as almost useless in equipping her for a practical role in life. In fact, the most educationally worthwhile experience she underwent was one she organised for herself: a coach trip around Australia when she was twelve. She talked at length about the impact of that trip on her thinking. The experiences on the trip—and the fact that she organised the trip herself—have had a crucial impact on her self-perception. She sees herself as unique and distinctive, and also as a person who makes things happen. She contrasts herself with her school peers:

Some of my friends from school have got jobs and they don't seem to have grown up at all. They're sorta straight from school. Like it's been drummed into their heads: 'Straight from school, you've got a job.' And they just haven't learned about life at all, they haven't got out and travelled...

They just stay with their own friends from school. They just haven't grown up. They just have babies and just do all the traditional things...

I haven't had things different, I've made things different and I've been taught the traditional way but I won't listen to it now. I'll do my own thing... Like I like being different, people are really amazed by me, 'Gees you've done a lot'... I just like being different.

The next significant event in Debbie's life was leaving home at fourteen. She boarded at first with a woman who 'hassled her about jobs'. Her response was to leave and then, as she saw it, she 'got her act together' and developed a 'macho image':

> Like I got this real big macho image and it's really good because—I'm not really macho at all—but people listen to me and not walk over me when I'm macho. Like if I don't like someone talking too much I'll say, 'Shut up before I hit you' or something like that.

When Debbie moves into a refuge, this macho image comes into play:

> I came here and I took control. Cause I sorta control the kids. I've sorta lived a bit more than them and they sorta like to hear about my experiences, and stuff like that... They don't give me any cheek at all. And I say, 'I'm pissed off with you and I'm pissed off with you'. And I tell them what I think all the time.

Throughout all these episodes Debbie is presenting a particular self-image. She sees herself as more worldly and more experienced than her peers. Travel features prominently in this: '...they haven't got out and travelled...' and 'I've sorta lived a bit more than them...'. She also sees herself as a self-determining person, someone who controls the people around her and also controls the social environment: 'I haven't had things different, I've made things different and I've been taught the traditional way but I won't listen to it now, I'll do my own thing.' Debbie conceives of that environment in the narrow terms of being told what to do. The more subtle and yet profound ways in which her social environment has shaped her go undetected.

The ideology of individualism is never far away. This ideology defines people in the same way that Debbie defines herself: as a self-determining individual, entirely responsible for making things happen. For example, if people are poor or homeless, then that's their fault for not doing something about it.

This image of a self-determining person, very much in control, is a self-perception which allows Debbie to maintain her macho behaviour and to be assertive and aggressive in defending her interests. Here is how Debbie confronted the Department of Social Security[17] when she was too young to be eligible for the dole:

> I tried to get Special Benefits[18] for ages and ages and at that stage mum and dad didn't want me back home. It took me so long to try

and get it. They didn't think my case was good enough.

So I just went into Social Security one day and I felt so much outrage. I just thought about it so much I got myself worked up in this rage. And I told them how stupid they are and how they're a pack of fuckwits. And I gave them heaps. And about a week later they came around with a cheque for me.

Later, when on the dole, Debbie's cheque failed to arrive, so she went into Social Security again:

> I went to get a counter cheque and they wouldn't give me one. They wouldn't believe me so I sat on the floor of the Social Security office until they gave me one... They started threatening me, 'We'll have to get people to come in and get you out.' And all this bullshit.
>
> But I just sat there and said, 'I'm not moving...' And from now on, from then on, when I want a counter cheque, I get one.

Whether or not Debbie's actions were really effective in each of these episodes is difficult to know. She herself clearly sets up a cause-and-effect version of her actions. Whatever the case, it is important to realise that Debbie is dealing with a welfare agency for whom she is—officially anyway—a client, and she thus has certain rights.

When it comes to the job market, Debbie's standing is quite different. No longer a 'client', she is now simply a person with nothing to sell but her unskilled labour power. In this context, Debbie's mythical view of the self-determining individual continually runs up against the real world of employer's power and stultifying work. Here the experiences are of defeat. Debbie left her first job because of sexual harassment: her boss 'couldn't keep his hands to himself'. After that there was a three-day job at a chain store ticketing clothes. This was followed by a job at a roller-skating parlour and her last job was in a fish-and-chips shop.

In all these situations Debbie had no control over her working conditions. Her only option when things proved unsuitable was to leave. But this was no real freedom since, in a climate of high unemployment, to continually leave jobs is to condemn oneself to a dole-queue existence. Debbie does not perceive how redundant is the idea of the self-determining individual in the world of work where unskilled workers have such limited freedom within a set of unequal power relations. Instead, she sees the situation in terms of her own characteristics: 'I can't explain why I don't like work, I'm slack, put it that way. Not slack, I...[searching for the word]'.

The increasing periods of unemployment which begin to fill Debbie's life revolve around an increasing dope addiction—'Well I'd prefer to get stoned all the time than go to work'—and a drifting in and out of places like the youth refuge. When she attempts to rebuild her family ties she finds it must take place on new ground. Her mother has remarried, which Debbie seems to resent. She expresses this in her belief that it hasn't worked out: 'Mum's remarried now, living very unhappily ever after...dad's just raging all the time.' As well as the remarriage, Debbie's dope addiction is a new factor, one which she sees as leading to lost independence if she stays with her mother:

> My mum couldn't understand why I didn't want to be with her. Like after I left dad, I went and stayed with mum, and she was just over-motherly. She was trying to make up for the years when she left me and everything like that. And I just didn't want that. I just wanted her to be herself, and just be my mum.
>
> Like I'd come home stoned and she'd freak out a bit and she'd say, 'Oh my baby', and make me some munchies and care for me and get out the stretcher bed for me. She just killed me with kindness and I used to say, 'Mum, stop it, slow down, slow down'. And then I just left and she wondered... And everytime I come around, she goes, 'Oh come and live with me. I love you, blah, blah, blah'.

During her time unemployed Debbie seeks male companionship, living briefly with a young unemployed man. Their friendship does not produce shared insights about their common plight but instead reinforces the depoliticisation so evident in chapter 3:

> We never used to talk about the dole much, He'd like to talk about it but I used to say, 'Shut up, I don't want to hear about it, I like being on the dole'.
>
> And he'd say, 'I want to get a job but'.
>
> I'd say, 'Go and look for one then'. That's as far as it would go.

As Debbie sees it, thinking only leads to greater confusion. She does not really see any value in reflecting upon experience: 'But I don't think about real life that much. I've done a lot in my life but I don't think about it.' When she finds herself in a protracted argument in our conversation, she soon senses that it is an unequal contest and she jettisons the discussion:

Debbie: I don't think you take from the rich and give to the poor. Like donations are really cool.
IW: Why not take from the rich?
Debbie: But the rich own that money, you don't own it. They own it.
IW: But how did they get it?
Debbie: They earned it probably. Went out to work and got it. They were born rich, inherited it. That's theirs. Why should we take theirs? Oh, make donations, that's cool... But nobody really goes starving in this country do they? You don't see people just lying in the street with big pot bellies full of gas... No, I just don't agree that you should take money from the rich. If they want to give money, that's cool. And they supply the jobs for the unemployed people. And they think, 'Why should I go and give money to these people off the streets. They've gotta earn it, sorta thing. They've got to work for it'. They don't just give money away. I don't.
IW: Where do you think the dole cheque comes from?
Debbie: The government.
IW: Isn't that being given to you?
Debbie: Yeah, but that's a different story.
IW: How?
Debbie: Not enough jobs around.
IW: What's the difference between rich people giving up their money to people like like yourselves and...
Debbie: Tax pays.
IW: Tax just does the same thing doesn't it? It's not a donation.
Debbie: It's not a donation?
IW: It's the same as your dad giving a whole lot of money to Steve here who then gives it to you instead of your dad giving it straight to you. What's the difference?
Debbie: My dad wouldn't give me a whole lot of money.
IW: And a lot of rich people wouldn't give poor people money except the tax makes them do it. But it's still the same thing, isn't it?
Debbie: But the government's got lots and lots of money.
IW: But they get it from people.
Debbie: But they spend... I don't like talking about unemployment because I'm not really interested in it. Maybe I'm unemployed but I just don't fit into unemployment conversations.

This conversation has simply reinforced Debbie's general rejection of discussion as a fruitful area of activity. She lacks the resources to make it an equitable exchange so she responds by vacating that domain. Debbie's experiences of schooling have made intellectual discussions, like 'unemployment conversations', an area where her self-esteem is under threat. Her response to this vulnerability has been to locate that self-esteem within another domain: physical activity. Debbie's 'dominance' in the refuge is not achieved through logical persuasion or even rhetorical flamboyance, but through her prestige in being 'worldly' and her threats of violence. Her success at Social Security came not through discussion but from taking action. Even in the passage at the beginning of this chapter, Debbie's response to the rapist was physical action rather than attempts at persuasion (which would have been ineffective).

In all these different episodes, Debbie has pictured herself as self-determining, assertive and independent. When the youth workers speak, a different picture begins to emerge:

Ruth: But with Debbie, you were saying about her being the advocate of free will and that. In a sense, that's a good observation in that that's what she would like. That's her ideal of being; even though what she does contradicts it all, it's still something she really longs to be. She'd be just thrilled to the eyeballs to be able to This is This. Decide something for herself. Cause something for herself instead of something else causing it.

She was very dependent on her mother. Even while she was here, she was trying to sort of get her mother to leave the guy, her present husband, and go and live with her so she could look after mum. But when mum went back to the husband, she was all teary and upset.
IW: She wanted to be with her mum?
Ruth: Oh, yeah, desperately needed her mum.
IW: She painted the picture that it was her mother needed her.
Ruth: No. I mean her mum probably would have liked to be with her. She was really dependent on mum and she would have loved to have lived with mum. She said that she had almost talked her mum into moving in and getting a flat with her, only mum decided to go back to the husband. I mean that really cut the kid up. She was really upset cause that was something she desperately wanted. Though she has a way of looking at things, for some reason admitting emotion or things like that, she sees as a weakness. She's not being strong if she says she needs something. So she goes to the opposite extent and says what she'd like to be, and I think a lot of them do that.

IW: The thing about being in control of her own life was a bit of a facade in a way too? She said she had learnt to learn from her hassles and was not going to have any hassles and she came across as a superconfident, much-in-control sort of person.

Ruth: Well, in a sense yeah. She'd said to herself, 'I'm not, going to have hassles', not, 'I'm going to learn to cope'. So she'd just go out fighting... Her bad temper would get her into more strife than it was worth. Her dependence on drugs would get her into trouble, like it has now. She's had to flee [interstate].
Stuart: Her dependence on this place too. After she left here, although it was really obvious that she wasn't good for this place [she was 'expelled' for using drugs in the refuge] and this place wasn't good for her, in her mind it was all a matter of personalities. Ruth was a bitch. I'd hardened up but at least I was still talkable to and so I was the one she came to. In fact, the first thing she asked me when she rang up was could she move back into the refuge.
Ruth: She didn't have control of herself. She'd say, 'I can't let myself cry, I can't let myself cry, because if I do I end up getting depressed and I try to kill myself'. You know, a hell of a control!
Stuart: Or, 'I've got to have my smoke. If I don't have a smoke of dope everyday, I'll just go crazy. I need it, I need it'. So she had all these dependencies. Without them she was reduced to less than a strong person.
Ruth: She always wanted a guy there too, but she wouldn't as much say that she needed someone. It'd come out sometimes quietly.
Stuart: There was an undercurrent of that all the time. She almost more than anybody was very dependent on having a boyfriend. And she was happiest when there was somebody who she thought was reliable and faithful, and she was unhappiest when she was breaking up.

As the conversation with Debbie drew to a close, it too finished on this theme. Debbie speculated about her immediate future and her current plans to move into a group house with a young man. She sketches a domestic scene which is clearly leading toward a pattern of dependence on, and subjection to, a male 'breadwinner':

IW: What does being equal in a relationship mean to you?
Debbie: Sitting at home, both on the dole. Drinking lots of bourbon and smoking lots of dope.
IW: Does it mean sharing out the work?
Debbie: Yeah, sharing out the housework, sharing out the cooking, stuff like that.
IW: A lot of women get into situations where that doesn't happen, where they do all the cooking, all the housework...
Debbie: The house I'm moving into with this guy, I'm doing all the cooking, cause I love cooking and he goes out to work. It's not what I

want, but that is what's gonna have to happen.
IW: Why?
Debbie: Because we won't be able to afford the house.
IW: Why can't he do his share of the housework?
Debbie: Don't worry he will.
IW: But you were just saying you're going to do all the cooking? Why can't he help with the cooking?
Debbie: Cause I like cooking. I wouldn't mind if he didn't help.
IW: But that's not being equal?
Debbie: Oh yeah, but he's going out to work and I'm not. I'm sitting at home.
IW: But you're paying your share of the house?
Debbie: Yeah.
IW: So what's it matter if he goes out to work?
Debbie: He supplies the dope... So I'll let him off on the cooking then.
Stuart: If you were going out to work yourself, would everyone do equal work then?
Debbie: Oh definitely!

Claudia's early high-school education was at a private single-sex church school, but her final two years were at a state school. After leaving school she too finds herself unemployed. It is, however, a situation which contrasts strongly with Debbie's. Claudia occasionally seeks work, but her awareness of her own self-sufficiency leads her to the view that it is probably best if she does not find a job:

> I tried for this job at a shoe store in town and I was twenty minutes late because I missed my bus. And the man in the shop was very, very angry at me because I walked in twenty minutes late expecting to find this job. And he'd had to answer to fifty women that had waited outside for hours...
>
> I would really feel quite guilty getting that job because my parents aren't pressuring me. They're quite happy seeing me race around doing all these things. And there are a lot of people whose parents are really on their backs about work, saying, 'You're really slack. You're a little layabout. Get a job'. And really having a hard time about it. So I'd much rather someone else got the job.

Claudia's 'racing around' is her voluntary community activities, mainly working at the youth refuge and working with handicapped children. She sees this kind of work as far more socially useful than most paid employment and finds, moreover, strong encouragement from her parents. If anything, they worry that she may burn herself out through taking on too many commitments.

Like Debbie, Claudia faces difficulties with unemployment. In her case it is the Commonwealth Employment Service:

Claudia: I don't particularly like being involved with the CES.
IW: The hassles of handing forms in?
Claudia: Not that, that's really nothing, it's really easy to do that. But the times that I go in and have to wait a little while I just listen to the noises around me and the things that are being said, and it's pretty depressing. Sort of, a whole lot of unemployed people just waiting to get a little bit of money and all these other people who have this terrible position of having to be like parents. I'd rather have to answer to my employer than this incredible mass that really knows what's happening to you. I just don't want to be on file when war comes. I'd rather be unknown.

Where for Debbie her experience with Social Security was a confrontation over the basic question of money and daily survival, for Claudia it is a question of a different kind of survival. What is at stake is her survival as a Person when forced to submit to the dictates of bureaucracies. Notice that as well as expressing sympathy for the unemployed ('just wanting to get a little bit of money'), Claudia also senses the plight of the bureaucrats ('this terrible position of having to be like parents'). Claudia has decisively moved away from analysing her situation in terms of personalities, of spiteful or petty officials intimidating her. Instead she focuses on the structural features of that situation, for example, the machinery of surveillance and control symbolised by the keeping of files.

This sensitivity to structural factors recurs in many of Claudia's comments. Behind her thinking lies a strong belief in the power of conditioning:

I feel that when we're born we're just a nice little bundle of niceness...just really really ready to take everything in. And then the things that get put into you are really really wrong and really mushed up so you end up, your brain just goes splut. [Hurriedly] I mean nice things happen too.

This belief allows Claudia to understand the lack of communication she finds in the world around her and to understand why she is constrained the way she is:

I feel that our society is a society that pushes for self-gain and self-improvement and the result is a whole lot of people in teeny weeny little cages and not being able to reach out to other people. And just when you sit on buses, and I know I'm dying to sit with someone and talk with someone, but everyone sits on their own little seats and just sorta feels really nervous and everyone's eyes are sorta keeping away. But it'd be so nice...

You know the other night I had such a good night because I just sorta met one person somewhere and I'm going to take them to the museum cause they're new in Australia and I'm going to do that. And I went to the local cinema and crept upstairs and talked to the man who runs the whole thing. And it was really great and everyone's really ready and happy to talk to people but we're just too scared. I think if I was peaceful inside, I don't think I would be as scared as I am of people and not as unassured.

Interestingly, Claudia seems to see the answer to this problem of conditioning as a personal one, not a structural one. She suggests that if one can find an inward peace, then one can begin to decondition oneself. This outlook seems to have grown out of Claudia's religious beliefs which emphasise personal tranquillity rather than political intervention as the answer to social problems:

If my happiness depends on the things happening to me in the physical world, then I might never be happy, or I could have happiness and then sadness... But if my happiness can come from the air, and live off life, just live off the fact that you're born and 'Wow' and live off that. Well you're always alright and it doesn't matter if things don't happen to you or they do, and you can get beaten, and it doesn't matter...

A potential contradiction underlies these comments. In one way Claudia's argument about conditioning implies that a person's environment is responsible for the kind of person she becomes. Yet the answer to deconditioning people seems to be to resolve the issues entirely within one's own 'heart' and ignore the omnipotence of the external world.

These sentiments take on a concrete form in Claudia's acquaintance with feminism. Her awakening to feminism resulted from a carefully engineered experience at youth theatre:

I go to youth theatre and we started workshopping feminism and suppression of women and all that sort of stuff. And I remember one particular workshop that someone devised got incredibly heavy. We had to do really hard labour, the men and the women together. Just to build this thing with chairs and then the person who was supervising, who was a male, kept telling us to smash it down, cause it wasn't good enough and to build it back up again.

And then he started, when we'd have our breaks from work, he d let the men have it easier and the women'd have to keep working and stuff like this and it got really really really heavy. And one girl, towards the end, just cracked completely and started screaming and crying and getting really hysterical and saying, 'Why, why, why? I get it all day, I get it all day. I'm just sick of it. God. Blahhh'. She went loony and ran out.

And I was really shocked because I didn't know what she was talking about and it took so much guts to say, 'I really don't know what she's saying. What's she talking about, she gets it all day. I don't see a thing. I think we're all equal'.

And they just said, 'Look, just start looking and you'll start seeing things'. And it just happened really quickly. I just went shshshsh. And it just keeps happening now. It's sorta slowed down a bit, but something'd happen, it'd hit me again with incredible sorta force.

Her religious outlook, particularly the emphasis on inward tranquillity, has made her feminism a very mildly political one:

If someone's really angry at me and I'm just loving back, well after a while they'll stop being angry. They might not. But just in my experience of doing this to people they really get taken back by it.

I used to hate, really hate a man if he whistled at me or if he was really off. I'd just feel so much anger and that anger is really negative. It just doesn't do anything. It just builds up a bigger and bigger gap.

The irony with Claudia is that her feminist perspective is a structural one, a perspective which transcends individuals and illuminates the social context which produces sexist social relations. Yet Claudia's feminist politics are very individualistic. In a way her religious beliefs overlie her other intellectual inclinations and give them a particularly spiritual dimension.

Claudia's feminist perspective allows her to come to terms with her own experiences, to reflect upon them and to draw out fruitful insights. The passage at the start of this chapter is a good example of this. Another example is her awareness of her own vulnerability to sex-role stereotyping. As she admits: 'The awful thing about it is that when I feel myself being attracted to someone, I just play the little female.' She understands, moreover, why this vulnerability exists. In the following passage, she reflects upon the gender socialisation which she experienced in her early high-school years:

> Horrible things go on. I hate that whole business of boyfriends, girlfriends. I can't cope with it. I hated it in fourth form. I tried so hard to be part of it in fourth form, and failed. I was never one of the 'chicks'. I couldn't make it, so I was desperately unhappy about the whole business. But the whole time, I'd write in my diary every night: 'Great day, lots of fun.' And go on about what a fun year it was. But inside I was really hurting because I wasn't making it.

Claudia's feminist perspective allows her to now understand and recognise the self-deception she was then practising. At the time, however, she experienced it as prolonged unhappiness produced by failure to succeed within conventional peer-group roles. When she moved to a co-ed school in her last two years, the sexism became even more extreme, but at the same time, the avenues out of it began to open:

> I tend to think there's a more balanced feeling at the single-sex school because it was more clear... I suppose there's a lot of tension because of that, and suppressed feelings and all the rest of that. It's not very natural being brought up with all these girls. But there's nothing nearly representing freedom at the co-ed school. I just think it's the most squashing, suppressed... How many other yukky words can I think of!
>
> It's incredible pressure at that school to be in your peer group, to fit into what they do. And there was only a small group of us who dared to go and step off the path a bit. And we got hell for it: 'Lesbians!'... The pressure to have your man, and to be a macho male. It's totally sexist, the whole business. And the guys were calling us lesbians because their egos were really wounded because we weren't getting into boyfriend–girlfriend business. They actually wanted us to go, 'Oh no, we love you desperately', so they could be real men. But we didn't do that, and so they continued to call us lesbians. It's just that we'd be really affectionate, and hug and roll around and wrestle and be physical. They'd never... only physical with your boyfriend or girlfriend.

The physical affection and emotional loyalty Claudia finds in these female friendships helps her break free from the sexist ideology which had produced so much unhappiness in early high school. Dismantling this ideology is still incomplete, as her comments above about 'playing the little female' show. However, the solidarity with other women which Claudia achieves in later high school has helped her break free from the destructive practice of trying to match a stereotyped *ideal*. Now her happiness flows from *real* relationships, such as the warm companionship of her female friends.

On the other hand, these males in her school are locked tightly inside the psychological prison of their narrow masculinity. Claudia's partial breaking free from her gender socialisation is at the same time a frontal assault on male socialisation. When these males scream 'lesbian' at Claudia and her friends, it is not simply a situation of intimidation or aggression. More importantly, their response is a measure of the fear these males feel in having their security undermined. This is really ironic. Trapped inside this ideology of macho masculinity, these males in her school lash out at challenges to their power. At the same time these aggressive actions constrain them even more firmly within the boundaries of a masculinity which is also oppressing them, preventing them from adopting less stereotyped behaviour.

Glancing back over these glimpses into Claudia's life, we begin to see several important things. Despite being constrained within an oppressive sexist ideology, Claudia finds the room to move outside this ideology and begins to establish her autonomy as a woman. This happens partly because the sexist roles don't 'work': they offer an ideal which is unattainable for Claudia and which ends in deep unhappiness. Her feminist teachers and theatre experience also play their part. They offer crucial insights which help shatter the myths encasing those sexist roles. Furthermore, Claudia's close friendship with other women provides the solidarity needed to exercise autonomy in a hostile world. And all the while this is happening, Claudia is secure in a social environment which is generally comfortable and supportive.

By contrast, Debbie's bleak schooling experiences, and her isolation from close friends with whom to share thoughts, have robbed her of the chance to dismantle those oppressive ideologies which fashion her life with so little autonomy. Moreover, Debbie's social environment is one of increasing dependency. Her poverty and homelessness have trapped her into dependency on a male, on drugs, on places like the refuge, and on her dole cheque arriving regularly.

The irony of this contrast is that Debbie, who possesses the least degree of real freedom and autonomy because of her vulnerability and dependencies, celebrates in her outlook the freedom of the unconstrained individual. Claudia, who achieves a greater measure of personal autonomy because of her friendship network and her secure homelife, adopts a view of people's almost total vulnerability to an oppressive and corrupting environment.

One has only to look back to the original passages to find this whole pattern crystallised. Though both women were equally vulnerable to male sexual violence, Claudia and her friend fled to safety in the family car, borrowed for the night. It speeds them away to a secure home where concerned parents willingly listen to their story. Debbie, on the other hand, finds herself in this predicament through being forced to hitchhike alone. In her situation of poverty and homelessness, hitchhiking is almost her only option if she seeks mobility. In escaping from this male, she is still vulnerable and, in fact, relies on another male to remove her from that situation. Despite the resolve not to hitch, her social environment has not changed, and so her poverty pushes her back to hitching: 'but today I hitched.' The whole cycle of vulnerability and dependency is set in motion once again.

Part III
Class and Schooling

7
'We back answer like crazy'

IW: Do you get bored living here in the Western Suburbs?
Nick: If we do we stay at home and save money. We don't spend money on boredom. Probably cause it's so hard to come by. Money. Whereas down there [a coastal high school] I got billeted out with this girl. You know I walked up to the place and it looked like a block of flats. My first impression was, 'Gee this is a big block of flats'. And it was just her house, it was so big. They had five balconies...
  She wanted ten dollars for the dance and her father didn't have any change. I went errrr, I was so amazed. He's probably got money rolling out of his earholes.

Nick, who spoke briefly in chapter 1, lives in the outer western suburbs of a major city. The architecture of his school displays the steady spread of population in the area. The main building is a long, low weatherboard structure, skirted by a verandah and with a courtyard in front. Behind this building and to the side are a row of steel-framed 'demountable' classrooms. Further back, nestled neatly beside the oval, is the pride of the school: a new brown brick assembly hall. All the streets adjacent to the school are lined with small white fibro houses. Their gardens are well planted, but there is a stark absence of trees.

One of my conversations in this school takes place with two young working-class women, Donna and Trish. Both are sixteen and both are in their final year at school. They live in an area with 40 per cent youth unemployment and with over 30 unemployed for every job vacancy. When pressed for an explanation of this, Donna and Trish voice the familiar dole bludger myth:

IW: What's your explanation for the high unemployment in Australia?
[Silence]
IW: Do you think about it at all?
Trish: Not really, I just accept it as a fact. I haven't really thought about it at all.

IW: You haven't wondered why it's like that?
Trish: No.
IW: Donna, what about you?
Donna: Not really, a lot. I haven't really thought about it all that much. I just wondered why... I reckon it's a lot lower than what it is because 20 per cent of the people just don't try. They leave school, their main ambition, like Sherry, she left school, she had a kid and now she's on the dole, and that was her ambition in life.
Trish: And she's got all this other stuff for having a kid so she's with about five people living in a house.
Donna: The kid's spoilt rotten so she doesn't have to worry about the kid so she can go out...
Trish: She goes out every night and someone else minds it. She's got it made.
Donna: That's her life. She left school, she had the kid, she lived with her boyfriend for a while. They split up. And now she's a dole bludger. You know, she just doesn't care about a job and it's the same with her brother. He gets a job every now and then...
IW: Why are those people like that?
Donna: I don't know. They've always been like that, haven't they? I don't know why.
IW: Do you think there's any link between school and being unemployed?
Donna: Yeah. I think there is because if you feel that while you're at school that you're incapable, then when you go out to get a job and that, you think you're incapable, 'Oh well, may as well not worry about it, heh?' So you go on the dole.

High unemployment has become naturalised. It has become a kind of permanent, and unquestioned, backdrop: 'I just accept it as a fact', as Trish puts it. Another youth, who lived in the inner city, commented in the same vein: 'I don't know why. It's always been there.'

Adults who have known times of full employment should pause to consider that for this generation of 15- and 16-year-olds, the last decade of high unemployment has covered all their maturing years. It is not easy to grasp the cyclical nature of unemployment if it always seems to have been there: the spectre at the end of the tunnel of schooling, the punishment awaiting the school dropouts, the threat which parents and principals level at their 'discipline problems'.

Consequently, when unemployment is naturalised in this way, the only avenue young people have for understanding the problem is to juggle with those things which seem to be variable: the unemployed people themselves. Thus the personal characteristics of individuals—of people like Sherry—become the primary focus in Donna's and Trish's account of unemployment.

When it comes to assessing their own prospects, Donna and Trish are quite realistic. They expect to be unemployed and they expect to come under strong family and community pressures:

IW: Do you think you will be unemployed at any time?
Trish: Probably.
Donna: Probably.
IW: And what will you do? Will you go on the dole?
Trish: No, if I go on the dole I get chucked out. My parents are kinda against it.
IW: Why?
Trish: Because they reckon that everyone's bludging off their money and I don't know, it's crap the way they look at things.
Donna: Dole bludgers you know.
IW: Do you get the same at home too?
Donna: Yeah. 'I don't ever want to see you on the dole cause you won't have a home here' and all that junk.
IW: Really?
Trish: They say it in a nice way but. [Laughs]
IW: So what would they expect you to do if you were unemployed? They'd expect you to stay at home and live off them?
Trish: Yeah.
Donna: Yeah. If we were unemployed they'd expect us to go out and look for jobs.
Trish: And leave at six in the morning and come back at ten at night. And if we haven't got a job in a few weeks they'd want to know why. 'Haven't been trying hard.'

Trish is now at school, nearing the end of fourth form. She had earlier left school at the end of third form, intending to enter the workforce. All she found were the frustrations of the fruitless job search. Here she reflects on that period of unemployment:

Trish: When I left school, when I *was* looking for jobs, not very often, but when I was, I went to somebody in the city and they said I lived too far away. And I got doors slammed in my face. Walk up there in the pouring rain, drip, drip, drip. Slam.
[Laughter]
IW: What was it like when you were looking for work?
Trish: Frustrating. I hated it.
IW: What made it so bad?
Trish: All the knockbacks you get. You feel you're too hopeless to

get a job and it brings you down a bit and then your parents lay all this crap on you and then you feel worse.
Donna: Yeah. They say, 'You didn't do this right. You didn't do that right. Why didn't you do it the other way? You should have done this and you should have done that'. But you can't... It's impossible.

Despite this experience, Trish later suggests that the regulations covering unemployment benefits should be made stricter:

Donna: My brother, he'll be on the dole. He's already told me that, you know. He's not going to get a job. There's no way. He hates working. I don't know, it's just a matter of laziness or not wanting to get a job. See getting a job means, I mean why go out and get a job when you can go out and get the dole.
Trish: I mean you could have a rage all day and all night and still have money. I think to get the dole you should have to do more. Like anyone, I could go up there, sign a thing, leave school and go on the dole easy, just like that.
IW: You said before that after the first month when you haven't found a job, it gets you down.
Trish: It does.
IW: You're saying now you should be made to look for jobs, aren't you?
Trish: No, I'm saying to get the dole you should...
Donna: They should check it more because...
Trish: Anybody shouldn't get it. They should do something more than just walk up there.
IW: In your own case that would have made things hard for you.
Trish: But then I think it would have made me look harder really, in a way.
IW: But you were looking hard when you were looking?
Trish: I don't know. [Laughs] I was trying, but I wouldn't give a damn. I looked and if I got one and if I didn't, tough luck.
IW: Do you think if you looked harder, you would have got one do you?
Trish: I don't know. I can't really say, can I?
Donna: I reckon they ought to check it out more and make people look and harder there'd be a lot less unemployment problems. People just stand there and it's getting handed to them on a silver platter. They go down and sign their name and 'Blah, blah, blah' and the cheque comes in the mail and they just sit around and wait for it.
Trish: But just you think, just think Donna, if all a sudden something went wrong and all of a sudden you just got kicked out of home. Just say you had nowhere to go. And you couldn't get a job. What are you supposed to do? If you had to wait that long for the dole, You'd probably starve to death.

Donna: Yeah, I can see that too.
[Silence]
IW: Do you think there's an answer to unemployment?
Donna: No.
Trish: [Laughs] Cut out all the computers. Computers are pushing everybody out of jobs at the moment. It's stupid, I hate computers.
Donna: Computerising should be cut out a lot more.

The harsh criticisms directed at the unemployed in these comments are not only aimed at acquaintances on the dole, people like Sherry, but they also rebound against Trish for not trying hard enough herself. However, this self-condemnation is ambiguous. Trish isn't sure if it would really have made any difference if she had looked harder. Then, unprompted, Trish turns on Donna to argue a more compassionate line. The passage then ends with the first reference to something outside the area of the personal characteristics of the unemployed—a recognition of the new technology.

In this passage Donna and Trish are beginning to question the existence of unemployment. They had earlier admitted that they rarely thought about unemployment, but here they find themselves pursuing the issue at some length. In thinking the issue through, they have at their disposal all the usual community myths and prejudices, particularly 'blame the victim' attitudes and hostility toward welfare recipients ('handed to them on a silver platter').

All these prejudices surface regularly in Donna and Trish's homes where both parents take a very hard line on 'dole bludgers'. These prejudices are also fuelled by personal animosity toward particular individuals who have been unemployed, for example, Sherry.

But these prejudices and myths have to grapple with personal experience. Sometimes they work well and they end up being reinforced by 'yet another example'. At other times, they fail badly. Personal experiences may fly in the face of common assumptions and demand to be explained in new ways. It is no longer a simple matter of repeating stereotyped phrases but of confronting real problems. Trish must account for her own experiences: certainly experiences of 'not trying', but also experiences of rebuttal and frustration. The community prejudices lose credibility in this area and the sudden reversal, the eruption of compassion and empathy, testifies to the first cracks opening in this 'blame the victim' perspective.

Liberal reformers often hope that schooling can provide people with the intellectual tools with which to combat community myths and prejudices. However, it is naive to assume that because various enlightened attitudes are written into the curriculum, the people on the 'receiving end' will adopt these attitudes. Many things intervene between intentions and outcomes, particularly the social realities of schooling, what actually happens in the classroom and the playground. This is the area which educational researchers call the 'hidden curriculum': the host of implicit messages built into the classroom teaching practices and lesson content; the organisational procedures of the school; and the group dynamics of personal interactions.

The 'hidden curriculum' is organised around the same assumptions which underlie the ideology of individualism. From apparently trivial things like seating arrangements in classrooms, and competitive procedures on the sportsfield through to the way assignments are set and marked, the school promotes forms of behaviour which are strongly individualistic. Indeed the very idea of graded assessment relies on the assumption that educational outcomes are entirely the result of an individual's effort (and not the combined product of a number of factors, such as the kind of teaching and the nature of the curriculum.)

Several of the people in chapter 3 had been to an alternative school. In a way what characterised that particular school was that its hidden curriculum was largely out in the open. Its official aims proclaimed the goals of democratising education and empowering students by offering them as much autonomy as possible. Its classroom practices and its organisational procedures were also designed to facilitate these outcomes. Both Gail and Charles are evidence of the relative success of this progressive schooling.

For Donna and Trish, the situation is very different. Their school is only slowly awakening to the reality of unemployment. It responds with a few changes to the curriculum, mainly work-experience programs. But on the level of classroom practices and organisational procedures, their school plods on with the same inexorable routines. Knowledge is still organised around an academic curriculum oriented to university entrance. This makes most subjects irrelevant to the concerns of the great majority of the students for whom apprenticeships, clerical or service employment is the main destination. Lack of interest in learning is an obvious outcome. When this takes place in an authoritarian and hierarchical institution, official responses to such apathy are inadequate and so a cycle of conflict ensues. 'Discipline problems' is the way it is seen in official eyes.

In the view of educational researchers the situation appears quite different. Numerous studies in England have focused on how the working class experience their schooling.[19] They have found that working-class students quickly sense the irrelevance and debilitating nature of their schooling and many respond by resisting the official ideology of the school. The way these students resist draws upon the existence of a strong informal group identity among them. In finding a group basis from which to launch their forays against the official ideology of the school, these students are at the same time resisting the competitive individualism of the 'hidden curriculum'.

To teachers it sometimes seems that their students are being entirely negative, and are rejecting academic offerings which would be in their 'best interests'. But escaping into the ranks of the professional middle class through university entrance is a route only a tiny proportion of *individuals* can follow. The working class, as a *class*, cannot be upwardly mobile. And working-class students often know this better than their teachers.

Donna and Trish typify this process of resistance to the official ideology of schooling. They locate themselves within a peer group who deliberately set out to distance themselves from the school and its values.

Trish: They wanted to chuck me out of school cause I told my home science teacher off. She blamed me for something I didn't do and I can't stand that. I've got a very bad temper so I told her off. And she told our principal and everything...
Donna: You get in trouble really easy for back answering cause we're bad as each other. We've got rotten tempers. We back answer like crazy.
Trish: You don't mean to but after you've said it you realise, oo ah. But at the time you don't sorta think.

Resistance to the school, as an official institution, is carried over into the recreational side of their schooling. But the official ideology of the school fights back:

Donna: Like we're having a dance tonight...
Trish: 'No excessive petting or fondling.' [Laughs] The way they put

it really gets to you.
Donna: ...for ten minutes every hour or something...
Trish: So the lights go on and every one goes...
Donna: ...'so everyone can see each other and have a conversation.'
Trish: Have a conversation!
Donna: ...'because conversation's gone out of style.'
Trish: Only about half of the people, not even half that usually go, are going.
Donna: Because they don't like the new rules.

Resistance to authority is not confined to within the school:

Trish: We were supposed to go to court. We crossed a railway line and this railway guy comes up to us.
Donna: We got ourselves in more trouble then because we back answered and gave false names.
Trish: We thought we'd just give false names and leave.
Donna: But he kept us there and these security guards come down.
IW: Seemed a heavy reaction for just crossing a line?
Trish: Yeah, because we lied to them and we told them where to go.
Donna: The railway guy was real, real horrible. And we went, 'Yeah, righty oh mate. It's cool man. You know, don't worry about it'. The more we done it, the more he just got angry.
Trish: We were really calm, telling jokes and stirring him and everything.
Donna: And we leant up against this wall and he was calling the coppers and we're leaning up against this wall and he says, 'Get off the wall'. We goes, 'Ohhh, I'm sorry'.
Trish: 'Don't want to damage to wall.'
Donna: We're being real smart alecks to him. No wonder he called the cops on us. If I were him I would have too. We were in a mad mood, heh? [Laughs]

Donna and Trish's activities as resisters are directed against official authority. Where that authority violates their sense of 'natural justice', as in the classroom, they feel aggrieved. Where they know they are being provocative, they are more prepared to concede the morality does not lie on their side.

There is also taking place, at the same time, a resistance against *unofficial* authority. In stirring the railway guard, Donna and Trish are resisting the sexist ideology which dictates that they should behave as 'young ladies'. Instead of being submissive to this older, male authority figure, Donna and Trish are assertive, familiar ('righty oh mate') and sarcastic ('Don't want to damage the wall'). The other unofficial authority is their 'elders and betters'. The predominant *pedagogic* division in schools is between those who have certified knowledge and those who don't. The predominant *power* division, however, is between adults and 'children'. One of the ways in which schools maintain their authoritarian, hierarchical organisational structure is by continually invoking the pedagogic division to legitimate the power division. 'Sit still and be quiet, sonny, if you want to learn something' is a familiar example of this.

So, when as 'children', Donna and Trish 'answer back' to their adult teacher and when they stir this adult railway guard, they are unmasking and contesting a power relationship which insists on keeping them subservient. In resisting this subservience, Donna and Trish find powerful artillery within their peer group. In particular, sex and drugs are guaranteed to offend adult sensitivities. Yet as well as a defence against adults, the peer group is ironically also a prison of conformity for these young people:

Donna: And the pressure of drugs. 'Come here Donna and try this. Go on just try it, just try it.'
'Oh what the heck. Oh alright.' You know. You know you don't know what you're doing after that. You just tag along behind everyone else and everyone else tags along behind everyone.
Trish: That's one thing I didn't give in to was drugs. I've never taken drugs.
IW: How did you resist? How did you cope with those pressures?
Trish: I don't really know.
Donna: She just used to sit there and...
Trish: Stare at the wall or something.
Donna: I reckon she's a better person now because she stuck by what she believed in, whereas I couldn't...

And we talk. You need someone to talk to. I mean I feel sorry for the people out there that are on drugs and haven't got anyone to talk to because for them it must be pure hell, hell.
IW: You said before that the little problems became big problems?
Donna: Like you fail a maths exam and your father's relying on you to pass this maths exam for such and such... and it used to worry me, 'What's dad going to say?' Or I might have a problem with a boyfriend and this little problem with some boyfriend becomes a gigantic problem in my own mind. Or you'll tell it to someone else and they'll think, 'Is that all she's worrying about?'

and

Donna: Like peer pressure and everything comes on and you think,

'Oh this guy, everyone likes this guy and I've got him here and now. You know, and he's asking me, so why not?'
Trish: And you go back to school, 'Guess what I did...'
Donna: And then you can go [Pats herself] cause I got so and so. But then a week later so and so's got so and so and you go *zzzzzz* [Indicates a crash].

The adults most offended are, of course, parents. In both the areas of sex and drugs these young women find themselves at the intersection of opposing messages. Staying cool within the group conflicts with parental admonitions, particularly those about virginity:

IW: Is there much peer group pressure?
Donna: You're still a virgin and that's a real pressure.
Trish: Used to bring you down.
IW: Is the message from your parents to stay a virgin till you're married?
Trish: Yeah, very. My mum used to call me a tart all the time.
IW: Why?
Trish: Because I thought I was pregnant once and I don't think she appreciated it very much. [Laughs]
IW: How old were you then?
Trish: Fifteen. And she sort of put a lot of pressure on me and she told me she was very disgusted and I couldn't even look at her because she made me feel so guilty. I felt really terrible.
IW: She didn't have any understanding of how it happened?
Trish: That's right. She wouldn't talk to me about it. She said that she was disgusted in me and everything but she wouldn't talk about it, you know.

Unemployment and school performance are the basis for parental expectations, expectations which can form an insidious pressure. As was apparent above, drugs are one form of release from this pressure, but they are also an avenue which often traps young people inside another set of pressures.

The peer group, with its emphasis on sex and drugs, is a source of constant fear for parents. The means through which parents express this fear, considering they have so little direct control over their offspring's lives, is through the moral pressure of 'trust':

Donna: My father used to say, 'We've got a lot of trust in you. Don't break it'.
Trish: Yeah, my parents said that.

Donna: All the time you know, and that's all you get. 'We're trusting you, we're trusting you, we're trusting you'.
IW: Do they give you any practical advice?
Donna and Trish: No.
Donna: Dad used to say to me, if I got such and such a boyfriend, 'Are you having sex with him?'

'No dad.'

He goes, 'Are you sure?'

Trish: Are you sure! [Laughs]
Donna: And then when I did, he never asked me that. When I did really need me parents around, you know, they just didn't care because dad was getting drunk all the time. He was beating shit out of me and my stepmother. And my stepmother left and there was a great big hassle, halloo at home. It puts a lot of pressure on you there as well because you look for security somewhere else...

If I were to have gone home and said to dad, 'I think I'm pregnant', he would have gone, Boot, you know. 'You're no daughter of mine.' That would have been it.

Donna: They're very trusting.
Trish: They trust you so much. It's unbelievable.
Donna: You know, 'You sure you went to school today Donna?'

'Yeah. I went to school today.'

'I didn't see you at the shops this afternoon.'

'Probably cause I went straight to the station.'

'Do you usually go straight to the station?'

You know, the cross examining all the time. It really gets on a person's nerves.
IW: So they don't really trust you at all then?
Donna: No, they don't.
Trish: But they say they do to make you feel guilty if you do something wrong.

When Trish runs away from home, her father pursues her and all the parental fears come to a head:

Trish: Me and my girlfriend ran away from home...and me father knocked at the door. Everybody jumps. I hid in the closet and when he come in he finally found us and everything.

And I tipped a cold cup of coffee down the sink. He reckons it was drugs and he named all these drugs to the cops. He told the cops that I had it off with all the guys up there. And I was a virgin and I got very hurt and I told him never to speak to me again.

Donna's home life has been as unhappy as Trish's. Her father has divorced once already and his second wife has also left him at times. As mentioned earlier there is also a climate of drunkenness and violence in the home. Not surprisingly, Donna's family life has not offered any kind of base from which to resolve successfully the pressure of schooling and the peer group. Unlike Janet, who spoke in chapter 5, when Donna brings the question of marriage to mind, it is not to explore the range of her feelings. It is to give vent to a well-established conviction. She declares without reservation that she will never get married:

IW: Is there a reason why you've come to feel like that?
Donna: Well my parents are divorced. And my aunty's divorced and uncle's divorced and everyone near my family is divorced. I've got so many steps and that in my family it's unbelievable...

My grandparents of about 50 years have just divorced. That's a long time for two people to be together and then split up. It's taken a toll, a terrible toll on both of them.

Ten years, even ten years is a long time to be married to someone and then suddenly decide you don't love them anymore. 'I love such and such across the road, you know. I don't care about you anymore. Goodbye.' And it's all written down on a little piece of paper like this and you think, 'Oh heck'.

Unlike Janet, for Donna the institution of marriage is bankrupt. It is not a question of the people involved. The weight of numbers forces attention away from the individuals and towards the institution. The point where this realisation comes is the same point where the real hurt lies: the discovery that an institution, regarded so often as natural, is in fact only arbitrary, merely a social creation. This is crystallised in the phrase: 'a little piece of paper'. Divorce is a little piece of paper which ends 50 years of loving. Donna remains angered and perplexed by the disintegration of the ideal of romantic love, by the shattering of the mantle of naturalness which has descended upon this *social* institution.

This trauma could be the start of something positive. It could signal a liberation for Donna from a patriarchal institution which is designed to ensure her domestic subservience and thereby limit her autonomy as a person. But it is only the ideology of individualism which pretends that people's intentions are always realised. Despite her resolve, Donna's actual social conditions of daily life are likely to undermine her purely intellectual intentions. Young working-class women, like Donna, are not only vulnerable to the worst excesses of romantic ideology, but their lives are marked by a pattern of early marriage and motherhood.

Donna is unlikely to find support among her peers for this resolution never to marry. All the pressures which assail them will continue to assail her. In the long run, Donna's pledge may well be a hollow one.

8
'I wanted to get some discipline'

Lewis: Some stuff in maths they teach you, you'll never use. Like Pythagoras's rule and all that.
Steve: Area of a circle.
IW: Why do you learn these things?
Lewis: So you know them if someone asks you.
Steve: If someone comes up in the street and asks, 'Do you know the area of a circle?' [Laughs]

Steve and Lewis attend the same school as Donna and Trish. Like them they sense the irrelevance of much of their schooling. Unlike them, they have not responded through resistance. Instead they have evolved a strategy of pragmatic instrumentalism. They are prepared to tolerate the worthless aspects of their schooling in order to achieve their specific goals: gaining apprenticeships.

Lewis thinks he would like to be an apprentice mechanic, a worthwhile job because of the pay and because 'you can do your own jobs on the car, cause they charge a fair bit'. Steve wants an apprenticeship because he sees it 'setting himself up for life'.

School for Steve and Lewis is a place to have fun with your mates, but also, at the same time, a place to stake a claim on the future:

Steve: You have your mates here...it's good fun, it's a ball. You have things like school dances. You muck around at school, do your work together. It's really good.
Lewis: People reckon, 'Oh it's no good'. They're only the deadheads that are going to go out and just be on the dole. You've got to have a future to look forward to. So you learn what you can.

The 'deadheads' are either the school resisters or the dropouts, the people Lewis and Steve see populating the dole queues. In the following discussion, Lewis and Steve refer to these people, but they offer reasons for why they are like this. Also, like Marg in chapter 1, they blame the government for unemployment:

IW: Do either of you think you'll be unemployed at any time?
Lewis: Yes, everyone will. Everyone has to be unemployed.
IW: Why are you so sure?
Lewis: Well look at how many people are unemployed now. Look how many... GMH just shut down 15 000 people.
Steve: Like I know somebody who left school last year and is still looking for a job.
IW: What's the reason for the unemployment being so bad?
Lewis: The government.
Steve: Oh, it's not really the government. There's jobs out there, they just don't want to look for them. Plus they mainly want experienced people.
Lewis: They expect the jobs to come to them.
Steve: Most people on the dole now are the ones that have just left school. And they don't worry about that really.
IW: Those people you know who left school last year and are still looking. Why is it they're still unemployed?
Lewis: They're not looking hard enough.
Steve: Like they don't want to do an apprenticeship now. If you get into an apprenticeship now you're going to have good fun in the future. I read in this magazine, this bloke got this school together. One did apprentice. One was electrician, plumber, bricklayer. And they all met and they all built a house and sold it for so many thousand. That's what a lot could do together.
IW: Are there enough apprenticeships around?
Steve: There's a lot around. Especially the army, navy, airforce, are mainly the ones where there are a lot of apprenticeships.
IW: Why don't those people go into them then?
Steve: The probably couldn't hack the drill or being told what to do. Like we know the basic stuff cause we've been in cadets. Told where to go, what to do. A lot of people wouldn't be able to hack that.

. . .

Lewis: There's jobs around. If you look in the paper there's jobs advertised. Most of them want school certificate or experience. If you want experience you got to get an apprenticeship first.
Steve: You got to be in that field first.
Lewis: Most people that have left school last year and are still looking for a job, they're not looking too hard.
IW: You know some like that?
Lewis: Well, my brother, he's left four years ago and he's been on

the railway twice, I think. He's left... he was sacked once I think and he left once.
Steve: Whereas his other brother, he's on the railway and he's got his head screwed on the right way and he's going for trainee engine driver and he's pulling in 500.
Lewis: And my other brother, he's been on the garbo runs, he didn't like it, he goes off it.
IW: Why is he like that?
Lewis: He reckons the job should come to him and he shouldn't go to the jobs.
Steve: Whereas Richard's totally different, he'll make a go of it.
Lewis: Whereas Danny, he's just a bummer.
Steve: A no-hoper.
IW: Why is he like that and one brother like the other?
Lewis: I don't know. Danny's just got in with the wrong crowd I think. His mates, they're all freaks, stupid. They're just bludgers, that's it.

IW: Lewis, you mentioned the government being responsible for unemployment. What did you mean?
Lewis: Well, most of them, they're shutting down foundries. Like one I saw in the news a couple of weeks ago. They're shutting it down cause they want to sell it. There was 300 people employed there and the government wanted to sell that foundry and they won't let them. So if they do sell it, see, there goes all them jobs. So I think it's mainly the government that causes unemployment, not the government itself, but Mr Fraser, the drongo.

The tale of the two brothers and the references to deadheads show that Steve and Lewis still operate with individualism. However, unlike the people in chapter 1, Steve and Lewis are aware of the wider dimensions of unemployment. They show a sober appreciation of the climate of closures and sackings which characterises the manufacturing sector. They are acutely aware of how unemployment highlights the vulnerability of working-class existence. To combat that vulnerability, Steve and Lewis develop their pragmatic instrumentalism. If they can gain apprenticeships and become tradespeople they will be insulated from the impact of future unemployment. As Steve's example suggests, they even see the prospect of combining with other tradespeople to create employment.

In Steve's and Lewis's eyes, the apprenticeships are not for everyone. The 'deadheads' will clearly miss out. And as the openings shrink, only the armed forces' apprenticeships remain.

To gain them, a person needs discipline, in fact, the kind of discipline which Lewis and Steve just happen to have because of their cadet training. The logic behind this whole line of thinking grows out of a merger between the present and the future. Their emotional investment in a future apprenticeship serves to justify their current commitment to school and their involvement in cadets. Because of this, it is hard for Steve and Lewis to understand the reasons for resistance by their school peers, those who see only 'No Future' emblazoned ahead of them.

Family experiences are the main source for Steve's and Lewis's knowledge about the world of work. School offers a work-experience program, but that is only for fifth- and sixth-form students and Steve and Lewis will be leaving at the end of fourth form. If anything, school and the unrelatedness of much of the academic curriculum acts as a reference point against which they can work out their priorities. They are only really concerned with *practical* matters:

> *Steve*: My brother. Like my parents said, you know, 'You can do what you want to do. You can leave at fourth form or go through to sixth form. It's your choice but it's best to leave at fourth form and get an apprenticeship. You know, you set yourself up for life'.
>
> He was doing really well and he went through to sixth form. He started at a real estate, property manager. They sacked him. They reckoned there wasn't enough work and hired the boss's son. He was unemployed for a while. Then he got a job at the warehouse.
>
> My other brother, he was an apprentice carpenter and he was doing really well and he threw that in and he wanted to become a minister. So he's down at Geelong. Whereas me other brother, he was in the same form, he wants to do a carpenter and joiner. Like we all want to do something practical.
> *IW*: So all of you have influenced each other?
> *Steve*: Uh huh.
> *IW*: What about in your case Lewis, the same thing?
> *Lewis*: Yeah, just the same. Just get an apprenticeship, say mechanic, welder, sheet-metal worker, anything like that.
> *Steve*: All earn good money.

The reference to money recurs when they sum up what they want to get out of their future jobs:

> *Lewis*: A better future. More money.
> *Steve*: Happiness. Good money.

When asked why money was so important, Steve promptly launched into a discussion on inflation:

Steve: Like nearly every third week or so, something's going up and they reckon they're going to bring this down, bring that down. But it's always going up. So you've really got to get more money to live.

In their trajectory towards their future goals, Steve and Lewis continually define themselves against the 'others', particularly the 'deadheads'. This was apparent in their discussion about unemployment. Though they moderated their scorn for the 'bludgers' by recognising situational factors, Steve and Lewis still operated with individualism. Their conclusion still amounted to something like: everyone must face the prospect of unemployment, but those with their 'head screwed on the right way' can surmount this predicament, can resist the vulnerability and carve out a secure niche in this hostile landscape.

Among the group of 'deadheads', Steve and Lewis number people like Donna and Trish:

Lewis: There are some girls in this school who are a real pain in the arse. You know, they go around kicking at ya, spitting off the balconies. Like one of them spat on my uniform today. So I went and dobbed her to Lieutenant Jones. They're real little...you know.
Steve: Tarts.

By defining themselves against the 'others', by scorning the 'deadheads', Steve and Lewis are moulding for themselves a particular self-perception. Like Don, who spoke in chapter 1, Steve and Lewis see themselves as mature and responsible, heading toward a secure future through exercising self-discipline and sound judgment. Where for Don this happened by identifying with the academic curriculum, for Steve and Lewis, it happens by identifying with the school cadet corps:

Lewis: The first time I joined up in cadets I wanted to get some discipline, but there wasn't any discipline given out. You know, if you told someone to go and get...you know, they wouldn't say a thing. They'd probably take you round the back and give you a punch in the mouth or a kick up the arse.
Steve: Whereas if that back answering happened in the army, you'd be dead.
Lewis: You get taken around the back and smacked over the head with the butt of a rifle.
Steve: Whereas here, like here we can't do anything till...

Lewis: All you can do is put them on...
IW: Is that right though, to be able to beat someone up for being...
Steve: Not really beat them up, I reckon...
Lewis: It's discipline.
Steve: Like at school, if you do something wrong to a teacher, you get the cane, OK? Like here I reckon you should give them drill or something to stop them from doing it. We can't. There's orders that we can't do a thing.
Lewis: All you can do...
IW: How do you discipline them? What do you do?
Steve: Well you can't...
Lewis: You have to take the whole squad...
Steve: Like if Lewis was giving cheek to me, before I could take him out for a so-many-mile run or whatever. Now I can't do it unless I do the whole company or the whole platoon. Where the whole platoon could be doing nothing wrong and one kid could, and the whole rest gotta suffer for it. It's stupid.
Lewis: You can't give them push-ups, or anything like that or the whole squad has to get down and do push-ups.
Steve: Like the things we used to get. A boot up the bum and everything. Push-ups. I had to do 100 of them once. It didn't worry me.
Lewis: You didn't. You got someone else to do them for you. [Laughs]
Steve: I did about fifty of them. When you get told to do it, cause you done something wrong, next time you think about mucking round, you stop and think. You say, 'Nah, remember what happened last time'. Whereas they just keep on doing it... I put a kid on report five times but he's still in. Still mucking round.
Lewis: See, like giving respect to other people, they don't do it at school, at home. They don't give respect to their parents. But here they do, they have to give respect to all the lieutenants and everyone else that's above them in rank.
IW: You yourself said before that discipline was one of the things you wanted to get out of it. Did you mean yourself being disciplined? Were you worried you weren't disciplined enough?
Lewis: Yeah, that's it. No one's disciplined really. Most people are spoilt.
IW: But most people wouldn't say that.
Lewis: I know, they don't admit it. I do. Most people are spoilt.
Steve: Being in cadets, it rubs off on you.
IW: So you both think you're better people for having been in it?
Lewis: I reckon you stand heads and all above the people. If you see someone doing something wrong, you go up and do something right.
Steve: I reckon it kinda reforms you, really.

Lewis: If someone does something wrong, I know it sounds a bit stupid, say someone breaks a window or something like that, or kills someone, put them a week in the army with hard discipline and they'd soon learn.

At times Steve and Lewis talk about 'discipline' as if it is a commodity: 'I wanted to get some discipline, but there wasn't any discipline given out.' At other times, 'discipline' is synonymous with punishment. Their attitude to such punishment varies in the course of this passage. Initially they contrast 'proper' discipline with crude violence, yet a few moments later they approve of such violence. They then moderate this and restrict punishment to things like drill. Yet once again discipline and violence merge when Steve links push-ups with a boot up the bum.

The comparisons which are at the heart of this passage help explain these variations. One comparison is with the army proper, the domain of 'real' discipline. Here both the official discipline and the crude violence exist side by side. In a way, this example legitimates the idea that violence is an acceptable form of punishment. The second comparison is between their earlier period of enlistment and their present one. They contrast the violence they underwent when they were privates with the restraints placed on them now that they're officers. This difference frustrates them. They have finally gained authority but they have not gained the rewards which should go with it. After 'coming up through the ranks', the rules have been changed and the 'rightful' revenge on those now below them has been taken from them.

Activities which occur within hierarchical organisations are basically power transactions. In the cadets, for example, even though Steve and Lewis sometimes refer to it as a commodity, 'discipline' is not simply another skill like firing a rifle. It is actually an attitude, a particular kind of disposition shown by one person towards another. In the cadets, 'discipline' means deference to authority, respect to the those in the higher ranks. All the incidents of 'wrongdoing' which Lewis and Steve castigate are essentially violations of the power relations which underlie the hierarchy. The most obvious of these infringements are 'mucking up' and 'giving cheek'. These do not refer to destructive behaviour or anything similar, but simply mean not showing 'respect' to higher ranks. The same 'military' perspective easily encompasses schooling and the family, and Steve and Lewis criticise the same 'disrespect' and 'giving cheek' which they perceive occurring there. Because the existence and exercise of authority is rarely questioned in the military context, and because this domain begins to slide over into others, 'mucking up' and 'giving cheek' become universal moral labels for condemning what is basically resistance to hierarchical power relations.

The ideology of individualism lies behind Steve's attitude towards punishment. He universalises the deterrent effect of punishment on himself to argue that discipline can work for everyone, that it is bound to produce proper behaviour if applied firmly enough. In Steve's eyes people always act consciously and are in complete mastery of their actions and thus totally responsible for the outcomes.

By contrast, if it is recognised that the underlying basis of hierarchies is unequal power relations and that these are essentially oppressive for a large number of people, it is possible to arrive at a different conclusion from that drawn by Steve. Instead of his individualistic explanation, this structural perspective argues that people's behaviour within hierarchies is composed of complicated patterns of compliance and resistance to these unequal power arrangements. Their actions are basically survival strategies devised to cope with the structural pressures and constraints under which they find themselves.

Understanding human behaviour in this structural way requires that the oppressive nature of hierarchical power relations must be recognised. For Steve and Lewis, however, these relations go unquestioned. Like the family, hierarchies have become naturalised. The cadet corps is an area of personal experience where hierarchies operate most openly and where their legitimacy is most unquestioned. The automatic deference to authority which is meant to occur in the cadets provides the pattern for Steve's and Lewis's larger moral universe.

In reflecting upon the world of work, Steve and Lewis accept unquestioningly the rights of managerial authority. This leads them to condemn workers' collective actions, particularly the solidarity expressed through striking:

Lewis: One bloke goes and pinches something, right? And he gets the sack for it and the rest of the company'll go out on strike till they reinstate him. And that's stupid. Why couldn't they just let him go? He done the wrong thing.

Steve: One example, where my brother's working. This bloke he went off at lunchtime, he went down the pub, right? He's supposed to come back about one and he didn't come back till three. They sacked him and everyone went out on strike on it. And I reckon they should have just said, 'Leave. If he goes you can go too. He's done the wrong thing, not us'.
IW: Why do all his mates follow him out? Is it mateship?
Steve: Yeah. They go out with each other, and they say, 'Oh well, if he goes, might as well go as well'. Go out on strike to support him. Well, they shouldn't. He's done the wrong thing. It's his problem, not ours.
Lewis: He should be punished for it. Get the sack. If they stand up for him and they're stupid enough to stand up for him they should get the sack too.

This moral universe is one where the judgments Right and Wrong fly about quite freely. They are judgments which pay no heed to the various strategies of resistance to work discipline, to the basically unequal power relations between the bosses and the workers. Instead, in the same way that 'mucking up' in cadets is automatically Wrong, so too are the workers when they infringe on managerial authority.

Like Bill and Andy in chapter 2, with their union-bashing comments, Steve and Lewis suscribe to the individualistic outlook which entrenches the bosses' position and fragments the workers: 'He's done the wrong thing. It's his problem, not ours.' What goes unrecognised is that as members of the working class, Steve and Lewis could find themselves in exactly the same position one day. For workers, whose strength lies only in their collective action, it can never be simply 'his' problem.

Lewis has actually worked in a foundry for a number of weeks. His reflections on this experience take an identical form to the comments on unions:

Lewis: Down the foundry, it's dirty and noisy, but I didn't care. It was good work. I enjoyed myself. I got $148 for it.
IW: You're not worried about it affecting your health?
Lewis: I am worried about my health, too right.
Steve: Whereas I'd never go for a spray painter because I know you have to leave around forty because it gets into your lungs. As long as you never do something that really risks your health.
IW: If you're the same, Lewis, why are you thinking of those jobs? Cause they're not good for your health?

Lewis: Oh some of them aren't, but most of them are. Like a sheet-metal worker, he works in a foundry like my dad but he only has to pour the metal in. That's only working near hot metal. You know, you just sweat a lot. But in the foundry you have to work with dust. You inhale dust, you inhale dirt.
Steve: Zinc. Asbestos.
Lewis: You inhale the stuff off the metal and everything.
IW: All those people who do those jobs, is it right that they should have to take those risks?
Lewis: Someone's got to take them. Someone's got to produce the stuff. Someday it's going to be taken over by computers just to do it.
Steve: Everything will.
Lewis: Someone's got to do it. Why not them? There's a job there, take it.
Steve: They may like that job.
IW: But what if they said, 'It's not fair. Why should I ruin my health?'
Lewis: Well, leave it and get another one, a bit healthier.
Steve: What are those blokes like, those blokes doing the dirty jobs. Do they look really sickening?
Lewis: One bloke, the foundryman, not the foundryman, the furnace man. From the heat, it's made him all just saggy, baggy round the eyes and cheeks. It's not his health, it's just his...
Steve: He looks like he's half dead.
Lewis: Yeah, just looks like he's half dead from the heat, cause they're working near 40 000°.
Steve: Probably takes the energy out of you.
IW: Is it right that people should have to work in those kinds of jobs?
Lewis: Well someone's got to do it. It's up to them. If they like it, they can do it.
Steve: That bloke might like that job.
IW: Do you think the job has to be done? What would happen if we didn't have those kinds of jobs?
Lewis: Well we'd go without it. We'd have to go without it.
Steve: We wouldn't have chairs or anything, nothing made out of metal. The bloke who works in the furnace, they might like that job. Mightn't even be thinking of his health.

Steve and Lewis are by no means laissez-faire about their health. On the contrary, they draw careful distinctions between the different kinds of work and the associated risks. Their pragmatism is centred on the future and that means the future of their likely job as well. They intend to last the distance.

This pragmatism is enmeshed within the ideology of individualism. The answer to workers' health risks is not to restructure the workplace but for *individuals* to change: 'leave it and get another one, a bit healthier.' This individualistic response to a situational problem neatly fits in with the interests of the bosses. Steve and Lewis do not challenge the hierarchical nature of the workplace, where management takes no health risks, and where the workers have no direct control over their working conditions. When questioned on the need for such jobs, Steve and Lewis point out how 'society' would suffer—'We wouldn't have any chairs or anything, nothing made out of metal.' That the profits of the bosses would also suffer if the workplace was restructured goes unnoticed because capitalist ideology has convinced most people that the interests of 'society' are identical with the interests of the bosses.

Steve and Lewis typify that group of youths whom researchers in England have called working-class conformists: those who largely accept the official ideology of their schooling.[20]

This chapter has shown why this occurs. The commitment to school grows out of an awareness of the vulnerability of working-class people to high unemployment. To guard against that prospect they have developed a strategy of pragmatic instrumentalism, a careful policy of biding their time, developing their skills and personal resources and preparing for a secure future in an apprenticeship. It's not that they don't want to have fun; it's more that they're prepared to defer it for a future time, when their existence is more secure.

The experience of cadets fits in here. It is a kind of insurance policy and it offers experiences designed to provide 'discipline'. As Steve and Lewis see it—and indeed as many of the people in chapter 1 saw it—lack of discipline is one of the key characteristics of the 'unemployables'. Yet, the cadets is also the place where hierarchical power relations are legitimated, and in this sense cadets is also an apprenticeship into the world of work since those kinds of power relations predominate in the workplace.

The ideology of individualism cements all this in place. It reinforces the unquestioning acceptance of hierarchical authority and helps naturalise the ascendancy of the teachers within the classroom and the bosses within the workplace. Resistance to unjust situations is never legitimate because, within this perspective, it is simply defined as 'mucking up'.

9
'Ghettoes for the wealthy'

> The headmaster of the Anglican St Michael's Grammar School in
> St Kilda, Mr Tony Hewison, told the meeting that the cuts in
> government financing could turn independent schools into 'isolated
> ghettoes for the wealthy'.
> (Press report following the Labor government's 1983 reduction in
> funds for 41 of the wealthiest private schools.)

I have left the steel demountable classrooms and the fibro cottages of the Western Suburbs for the sandstone and ivy walls of an elite private school in the middle of the city. The driveway is heavily overhung by English trees, mostly elms and oaks, and leads up to a weathered sandstone archway with an engraved coat of arms and several flags fluttering. I pass through numerous courtyards, past several sports fields and eventually arrive at the small room where I am to talk with Richard.

Like Donna and Trish, Richard is disenchanted with his schooling. However, he does not openly resist schooling—he simply responds with apathy. Richard is also very different from the working-class women and men because he is a member of the wealthiest class in Australian society. He is the son of the managing director of a large manufacturing company.

Richard describes his own decline at school in stark terms:

> I don't have a great deal of fun here. I quite hate it actually, to be
> quite honest. There was a time, a long time ago, when I used to
> actually try and do exceptionally good. And then it kinda fizzled down
> to, try to do exceptionally good in the subjects that I actually like
> doing. And then it kinda broke down to, 'I don't really care'. That's
> how it is now sorta.

Despite this Richard persists. His brother stands as a warning of parental disapproval:

> And he used to go to this school and he did his HSC[21] here and failed

in every subject. So that really put him off with my dad. And that's when he left home.

Similarly, Richard's experiences of unskilled work, undertaken during the school holidays, contain a strong message about the wisdom of staying on at school:

> The jobs I did were pretty...manual sort of thing, no high-class jobs. I worked in the back of a removalist truck as an offsider for a while. The thing that made it really good was that you knew it was going to end in three months or so. It hung over your head that, saying, 'If I had to do this for the rest of my life, no way!' I couldn't do it.
>
> And it was good to come back to school, you know, and to think, 'Well, if I don't work at school, then that's what I'm going to end up being, a removalist or something like that'. And it made you work harder in a way.

So Richard puts in the hours and hands in the work, but he nevertheless deliberately distances himself from the ethos of his schooling. He finds support for this in a peer group outside the school. These are the friends who live in his home neighbourhood. Though he has a friendship group within the school, he regards them as immature and he emphasises that his outside friends are more important to him. This difference is highlighted in his comments:

> It's quite funny actually, I can talk to my friends at this school and say, 'If war came would you enlist?' and it's, 'What kind of question is that. Of course I'd enlist'. It'd be, 'Don't be stupid'. That'd be the way they'd think.
>
> But the friends that I muck around with on the weekends, my better friends, it's kind of, 'No, I wouldn't enlist. If it were made compulsory, I'd get out of it somehow'. It's quite funny, I don't know why.

Richard's own outlook on life pivots around a desire for wealth and the luxurious lifestyle which accompanies it:

> Well I guess one of the most important things for me would be to be very rich actually. You see my father was rich before I noticed that he wasn't rich, do you know what I mean. I've always known him as rich. So I've always had the proverbial silver spoon in the mouth so to speak and I don't know any other life apart from that.
>
> I mean I haven't been spoilt. Like I've got a motorbike at the moment but I paid for my motorbike by working. And my dad never used to give me more money than I would come to harm with, if you

like. But we've always had the best of everything, like go overseas, stay at the best hotels, eat the best food, go to the best places. Any other life for me I don't reckon I could take it. If I had to be a labourer or something for the rest of my life, I just couldn't. You know what I mean. It wouldn't seem right.

His friends outside school reinforce this outlook by sharing in the same ambitions and similar consumption patterns:

Richard: My friends outside of school, a lot of them have got the same interests as me. They want to get rich, for one. They want to eat the best food, drive the fastest cars, and go out with the best looking women, and that kind of thing. And we'll help each other to get that, kinda.
IW: You never wonder if those kinds of things are worthwhile?
Richard: Worthwhile? For their purpose I guess they're worthwhile.
IW: Well what is their purpose? To make you happy or what?
Richard: In a way. Yeah. I guess so. I mean I could have all that money and assets and things, you know buildings, and be at times, terribly terribly down. It's a different kind of happiness. You have clothing and food and shelter and everything as the essential items for humans to survive, kinda thing. Well having that kind of wealth, well at least trying to get it, it's like that. See, for some people it's to have just a normal meal, enough clothes to keep you warm and a bed to sleep in. That is happy, ace, you know.

But for us, for me and my friends, for us, to be happy like those people are happy with their basic needs, for us it'd have to be the best of this, this and the other. You know what I mean?

How does the prospect of unemployment fit into all of this? Chapters 7 and 8 showed that the working-class youths are highly vulnerable to being unemployed, but they were also aware of that vulnerability. For Richard, there is almost no vulnerability—his wealthy home and school environment effectively insulate him from the threat of unemployment:

IW: Do you think you'll be unemployed at any stage?
Richard: No.
IW: You don't? Why not? Cause a lot of people in sixth form about to leave are going to end up on the dole?
Richard: Yeah. I... I can see... I never see myself as not having a job. I don't know why. I just do. I've always...like since I was in about third form, every holidays, even during school times, I've always held down jobs, even just little jobs. It's not that I think that the dole is bad. A few of my friends are on the dole themselves, but I reckon it would be...very hard for me not to have a job, I don't know why.

> I'm not saying that because I'm boasting or anything like that but I don't know, it's... you know I might be proved wrong, but it's the feeling I've got. I've always... I know a lot of people, you know. If worst came to worst I could use my father's influence in finding me a job. There wouldn't be any troubles there but so far I haven't had to do that.

When most of his peers in the working-class schools will be down at the CES office registering as soon as they finish the year, for Richard there's a brief holiday and then a trajectory which ensures that insulation:

> Ultimately I want to go and work in hotels as maybe a manager, one day. But directly after I finish the exams I'm going to Queensland for a week just to relax, just to take it easy.
>
> Then we're going to come back. I'm doing a bar attendant's course at tech at the moment and we've got jobs set up in the local club as barmen as soon as we leave school. That's just as starters and then I might work at Mercedes Benz as a kind of detailer. Clean the cars, take them down to rego and all that.
>
> And I want to hold down about a couple of jobs for about six months or until I get a bit of money and then I'm probably going overseas. My dad's sending me overseas to do this course for hotel management in Switzerland.

This interest in hotel management has been consolidated by a recent work-experience program at school which placed him in a hotel for a number of weeks. Its deeper roots, however, lie in the wealthy consumption patterns of his family:

> Actually being inside the hotel, all air conditioned and nice carpets and all that. It's really, it's really good. I've been overseas with my parents and we've always stayed in nice hotels. It's always fascinated me for some reason. I don't know, I like hotels. I might own one some day maybe.

This wealthy consumption pattern has a strong hold over Richard. Not only is it embedded in his daily routines, his lifestyle at home for example, but it also dominates his thinking. For Richard, this wealthy consumption pattern is seen as the only, and the most *natural*, mode of living for himself and his friends. Having announced his ambition to be wealthy, Richard continues:

> *IW*: When you said you wanted to be extremely wealthy, I was interested. Why not just wealthy? What's the difference? I mean, is it the difference between half a million and a million, or what?

Richard: When I say extremely wealthy, I mean kinda millions. [Laughs] It's a bit far fetched I guess but most of my life will be trying to build up an incredible amount of money. I don't mean paper money. I mean assets and investments. Hotels, racecourses, things like that.
IW: But why? Once you get to half a million, does any more make any difference? Would you know it?
Richard: Yeah, sure.
IW: How?
Richard: If... I've always got this terrible thing about, I don't know whether it's my character or something but I just throw money away like it didn't exist.

It's just I think again it's rubbed off from my dad. He always used to give heavy tips and you know, the amount of money that's thrown away on nothing is, I don't know, it's fun, throwing away money, it's great fun.

Say we go drinking one night and there's poker machines or whatever and my friends, they might buy a few drinks, yeah, fair enough. And then they might start putting a few tens and twenties in the poker machines and if they get unlucky, they'll lose, you know, their $15 and they'll be really angry. For a couple of days after, they'll be kicking themselves. But with me I can, you know, lose money, throw away money on nothing, and it never seems to worry me. I don't know.
IW: Do you think having a lot of money's going to make you happy?
Richard: Oh yeah, sure. When I say happy, I don't mean I couldn't be happy without money. I mean I'd be happy because I've had so much money and I'd have a good time throwing it around, you know. Just doing things that I want to do, and having people bend to my will, and things like that. But money doesn't buy everything as they say... wives, girlfriends and kids, things like that, money won't solve those problems. Probably make it worse half the time.

Significantly, the reference to family problems is borne out in Richard's own case. His father has divorced twice and his family life has, in Richard's own words, 'collapsed'. Richard concedes that the family's wealth is a factor in this:

Richard: Then my dad got divorced from my mum. He got remarried and then they just recently broke up again.
IW: Do you think some of these problems are to do with wealth?
Richard: Yeah, you could say that. With his second marriage, the reason that broke up was because he didn't spend enough time with the family cause he was always going interstate and overseas. He had to move around a lot because he had to look after his own business naturally. Some people can understand that. I can understand that but

my stepmother she couldn't understand that...she couldn't understand that business should come before love and the family and all this kind of garbage.
IW: Do you accept it?
Richard: I accept it. It doesn't mean I'm all for it. But I accepted it when it happened to me cause I'd said, 'Fair enough. That's the way he thinks. OK, I can live with it'.
IW: You would not have had the same time with your father that a lot of other people have?
Richard: Oh yeah sure.
IW: You accepted that? You didn't resent it?
Richard: No. I've always seen...well our family revolves a lot around money, wealth, contacts, things like that and from very young I can always remember a time when my dad has been late or hadn't come home and he hasn't told anybody. I always seem to be able to understand why. Just accept it I guess.

Some people haven't. My mum, after they got divorced, she used to always ring me up and say, 'What are you doing?' I'd say whatever I was doing.

'Where's your father?'
'Oh he isn't here.'
'Do you know where he is?'
'No.'
She'd go completely out of her mind.
IW: Why didn't you stay with your mum when they broke up?
Richard: She didn't have enough finance to look after me. She was...dad's smart. He puts everything in his name. When they broke up, she had nothing, he had everything. Didn't mean he didn't provide for her. You know, he still gave her a house, gave her a car, set her into a job. But on the condition that I stayed with him.

Richard does not necessarily mean 'approve' when he talks about accepting his father's neglect. He simply means that he's come to terms with it. How that's happened, or even how well it has happened, is hard to know. Richard may well be reading back into his past the acceptance he has only achieved in recent years and thus he may be glossing over the real hurt of his early years.

Whatever the case, it is clear that the wealthy consumption pattern of the family has provided most of the rationale for this collapse of family life: 'our family revolves a lot around money, wealth, and contacts.' Richard accepts this as a legitimate trade-off. Indeed, it even provides him with a model for his own future life. The way his father, who was 'smart', secured the financial rewards of the marriage and all the leverage that went with it, stands for Richard as a model of his own future family relations. After all, 'smart' is a very approving label for such ruthless behaviour.

Richard is so enmeshed within this wealthy consumption pattern and so preoccupied with his ambitions to be rich that he actually transforms what would seem to be a situation of emotional neglect into one of emotional satisfaction:

IW: What do you do when you're by yourself? Who cooks?
Richard: I cook myself, sometimes I go out and buy something whenever I feel like it.
IW: You don't get lonely?
Richard: No, I don't get lonely. I don't mind. I quite like being in a big house by myself actually. You can start dreaming about the house you're going to have and how rich you're going to be.

The habits and aspirations which make up the pattern of Richard's daily life appear to him as the most natural thing in the world. They are the way things would have to be for him, otherwise 'it wouldn't seem right'. This perspective colours Richard's outlook in numerous ways. Though the school he attends offers knowledge about the world which could be organised in a number of different ways, for Richard this knowledge is shaped to fit this perspective of wealth and luxury. It determines what issues, drawn from the unlimited range of contemporary political and social issues, are allowed entry into Richard's thinking. This is apparent when Richard is asked about the future:

IW: When you think about the future, I don't mean personally, I mean generally, Australian society, where it's heading, are you optimistic or pessimistic about the way things are going?
Richard: What do you mean, Australia as a whole?
IW: Yeah, the way the country is, the way the society is.
Richard: I don't know, I don't really pay much attention to... really the thing doesn't come into my thinking, ...cause, ...cause I've been over to Europe a few times and found that Australia seems a bit lacking in certain things, you know.
IW: What?
Richard: Hotels, for example. [Laughter] The degree of luxury compared to other countries. Like you go to Singapore, you know, labour's cheap and all that. The hotels there are perhaps the best in the world. But come to Australia and compared to most places around Europe, they don't stand up.

Clearly, everyone's thinking is selective. Everyone pays attention to only those issues which are significant in their lives. The point about Richard, however, is that this selectivity is remarkably narrow and this reflects the narrowness of Richard's daily existence. Richard, his family and his friends are extremely insulated from the daily struggles of most working people, from the unemployment that the people in all the other chapters face, from the physical hardship that many of their working-class peers confront. The focus on wealth and luxury reinforces this insularity, screens out the world of ordinary people where the struggle for survival is a daily reality.

In the following passage Richard is confronted by a point of view which challenges this preoccupation with wealth and luxury. Richard responds sympathetically and engages in a certain amount of self-reflection. But notice that Richard does not offer any kind of rationalisation, but simply keeps repeating how much his daily life excludes these issues:

IW: Having all the money, like your father has and like you may have, means that there are a whole lot of other people who don't have much money. Doesn't that worry you, that inequality in incomes, that injustice of it all?
Richard: Around my little world, yes. I mean my friends, I mean I'll always help people I mean. But people that I've grown up with...like a lot of my friends aren't from rich families, things like that, and...if I ever got rich, naturally I'd help them like. But I wouldn't worry about people outside of people I know.
IW: What about all the people in the Third World? It doesn't worry you...?
Richard: No, it wouldn't influence me at all. I don't know why.
IW: It worries a lot of people, it sort of nags at their conscience, they feel guilty.
Richard: No.
IW: It doesn't for you?
Richard: No. [Laughs] Really quite stone-hearted, but no.
IW: Has it ever? Has it ever been in your mind or has it always been just excluded?
Richard: Well my... I grew up with my father being intensely racist if you like and a bit of that's rubbed off on me. To be worried about what's happening in the Third World, I couldn't.
IW: Because of that racism?
Richard: Yeah. I mean if I was so rich and I came to, 'Oh, I have to give some away'. Well then sure I'd, I wouldn't give it to just my friends. If I had that much money I probably would give it to, I don't

know, towards a family over there or whatever.

But, it doesn't really worry me. I don't know, I think a lot of it's to do with attitudes. I think a lot of people know, especially in this school, my friends have incredible selfish, I use the word selfish, I mean, that's implying that I'm selfish too, that it's all: You're Number One and you want to get rich, that kinda thing.

To anyone I don't know, it's kind of, Switch Off. I don't know, maybe that's a great fault, I don't know. It probably is, but I wouldn't... It wouldn't eat away at my conscience if I was rich and down the street lived somebody that came from the Third World that lived in a council flat on the breadline. It wouldn't eat away at my conscience at all. Maybe it's pretty heartless but...

The ideology of individualism which lies behind much of Richard's thinking—and indeed the thinking of most people in this book—is more than just an attitude. It is also part of the daily routine of their lives. For example, the long-term unemployed not only looked at the world individualistically, but their daily lives were privatised; they always faced the world as isolated individuals. The same is true for Richard. The routines and habits of his daily life, particularly his family's consumption pattern, means that Richard is living as a 'free' individual, someone whose personal existence does not depend on others or have anything to offer to them. With his friends, there is a network of common interests: 'We'll help each other get that.' But this is far from a collective interest: they are still individuals striving for individual rewards.

Richard's father's marriage broke up because of selfishness, because the family ties were based on extreme individualism, not on a collective sharing principle. Even now, when Richard's brother decides to drop in for a visit, it is not a warm family reunion, but a cool exercise in which each person asserts their independence:

My dad and brother, they get on OK. It's not as if they're not on talking terms or anything like that. You know, my brother might fly down and drop in. Have a drink. Maybe have dinner together. But that's it. My dad's not an affectionate man, if you like. He's never kissed or anything like that, his kids. It's hard to tell whether he's in a good mood or a bad mood with anybody. I mean in the family that is.

This same 'freedom' of the individual, free from any moral obligations or ties, reappears when Richard positions himself within the wider society. In the long passage above, Richard sees no real moral obligation towards others. If he is charitable, then that is because he feels generous, not because he has any real obligation.

The question of charity is largely irrelevant to Richard anyway. His main preoccupation seems to be with accumulating as much wealth as possible, even though he recognises that this may be at the expense of other social relationships or commitments, 'wives, girlfriends and kids', as he puts it.

Again, sexist ideology nestles neatly beside the ideology of individualism. This sexism played an important role in the collapse of Richard's family life, in the way the needs of the wife and the child were rejected in favour of the needs of the husband, in the way the emotional ties of the family were replaced by instrumental ties. The same sexism lies behind Richard's approach to future happiness: he classifies women along with cars and food as objects for consumption:

> ...eat the best food, drive the fastest cars, and go out with the best looking women, and that kind of thing.

The family is the original site where Richard encounters individualism and sexism in a major way. But his elite private school is also crucial in reinforcing these ideologies. There is a close harmony between home and school. Not only do his school friends share the same ambitions for wealth and luxury, but the academic curriculum is aggressively individualistic. As two of Richard's peers commented, when discussing the role of competitive assessment:

> *David*: No, hang on. OK in economics right, Mr Bligh gives us back our essays right, and what happens in class. 'What'd you get so and so, what'd you get so and so?' And they want to know who they beat. That's it. That's how it is.
> *Andrew*: Well, OK, if you didn't have any assessment, you wouldn't have people knowing whether they're better than anyone else.
> *David*: That's right.
> *Andrew*: How depressing it would be for everyone who wants to know.
> *David*: But they just want to boost their egos, 'Look I'm better than him. I'm tops'. That's it.

Outside the classroom, the same process is in place. As I leave the school I pass through one courtyard where a regiment of cadets is drilling. All stand rigid, rifles at their sides, the sun beating on their backs. One cadet, affected by sunstroke, is led away into the shade. His peers smirk silently, then straighten themselves even more rigidly. I pass the playing fields and the same competitive and aggressive behaviour is also in evidence: a group of diminutive first formers hurl themselves after the ball as they go through their rugby training.

10
Conclusion

John is nineteen and was unemployed for eighteen months. During that time he lived in various group houses and worked in a number of temporary jobs, mostly unskilled and underpaid. He has recently enrolled in an alternative school, and though he has only been back a few weeks, he already notices a great many differences from when he was last at school. Now he is confident about finishing school, though not at all optimistic about finding paid employment afterwards. What he seems to value most are worthwhile human relationships, and he is finding many of these at the moment. John is a useful person to look at in this conclusion because many of the themes from the early chapters resurface in his biography.

John looks back on his earlier schooling as 'pretty dreadful...a big mass of fear and hassles'. He finally left school, midway through fifth form. This coincided with leaving home, moving into a group house and going on the dole. In his time unemployed, John lived in four group houses and worked in several short-term jobs. Mostly he was on the dole:

> Every now and then you get down until you're down in the dumps and then you sort of hassle around in your little quagmire till you're just fed up with the filth and muck and starving to death and you think, 'Right, I'll go and get a job'. And you tear around again for a few more weeks, waking up at six in the morning, licking people's boots...

It is the same cycle that Bill and his friends go through. As chapter 2 showed, the effect of all these knockbacks is a severe blow to self-esteem:

> You feel like you're a parasite or you're made to feel like you're a parasite even though it's not really your fault you can't find a job. After a while it tends to get worse and worse, just the futility of it all.

You tend to become really apathetic and then people can justifiably call you a parasite.

John however, refuses to accept this self-blame and directs his anger outwards:

> It makes you angry and resentful... Just the fact that you're yourself and you've got to live with yourself, got to try and keep a bit of an ego. If people are crapping all over you and hiding behind a form or a pay package, it just makes you angry and it just builds up inside you.

He even finds a ready target for his anger:

> It really makes you resentful. Like I call public servants fat cats and everytime a Mercedes goes by I laugh loudly if the window's open. And this government, things like that, hating Mr Fraser.

In directing his anger outward, John shares some of the attitudes common in chapter 3. Like Gail, he has an acute awareness of the stultifying conditions and the futility of the work which is currently valued in society:

> I'd die in an office. I wouldn't last a week. I never get up in the morning. I stay up too late at night. Working five days a week seems like selling your soul.
> 'If you give me twenty bucks I'll give you this nice sunny day that I coulda had sitting by the river or running around doing something. And I'll shuffle these meaningless pieces of paper around pretending that I enjoy it.'

The alternative though, is unemployment. Here John faces the same poverty and hardship seen in chapter 2:

> It's sort of a continual downhill slide really. There's a cafe in town which gives credit and you go and get a hamburger if you're without food for a couple of days. And you can go around to fruit shops and ask them for stuff they don't want anymore. You explain that you haven't got any food and that if there's anything that they're going to chuck... You can usually salvage a fair bit of stuff out of that... Try and get yourself invited to dinner somewhere.
> Clothes you can usually get at Saint Vincents. Or go snowdropping. Go stealing people's washing. You just look for a house with a Volvo out the front. They won't need this T shirt. Beauty. Things like that.

Living in a group house minimises the physical hardship because the living expenses are shared more economically. However, the depoliticisation discussed in chapter 2 was still the pattern for John's group. Though they talked about unemployment and shared their experiences, the outcome was still a sense of futility:

> We generally blamed it on America, just sort of sucking the profits out of Australia. I felt the more I heard the less I knew really. I just heard so many conflicting ideas. Someone's lying somewhere. Sorta bugger it, take another swig of the flagon.

It's not that John and his friends blamed themselves for their situation. Their gaze was outward and was critical— 'America...sucking the profits...'—but there was no obvious political path offered them. The strategies for social change were so conflicting, and the powerlessness of being unemployed and in poverty was felt so strongly, that there were simply no positive options available.

However, like Claudia in chapter 6, John became involved in youth theatre and slowly the picture became clearer:

> Youth theatre has helped me...in not being afraid to exist. It's helped me to see things and think things out. Rather than just get told things and believe them, I can actually come to a conclusion myself... It sort of seems to be a mirror for what's going on. You can play back, imitate people. And you can talk to people there all the time, things like that.

A good example of this is John's sensitivity to other people's perspectives. It has been noted in several chapters that people often operate with a 'self' and 'other' distinction and that sometimes the way they stereotype the 'other' prevents them showing understanding or sympathy. Notice below that John uses the same distinction, but that he is aware of doing it. Moreover, he thinks about how he must look in others' eyes:

> Everyone has their 'It' I suppose, like I've got fat people in Mercs, I blame things on them. [Laughs] I'm sure that when they drive past they're the bureaucrats that have buggered it all up and they've got it all stashed in a Swiss bank somewhere. And I'm probably their 'It'!
>
> You walk into Woolworths to do your shopping and you've got ten bucks for your week's groceries cause you've blown your rent and things like that. You walk in and there's people buying great fat portions of ham and huge juicy steaks and they look at you as you go past and they go, 'Tsk, tsk' as you're buying bean sprouts or something like that. And then you sort of go, 'Why'd they do that for?'

So it'd start to get to you after a while so you walk around and go
'AHH AHH!' as you walk past them. It's just a question of people
just not communicating. Like that person was probably quite nice.

As well as sensitising John to other people's feelings, youth theatre has also opened has eyes to how rampant sexism is in contemporary society:

Theatre is a very useful thing for demonstrating sexism and showing
people that. Like there's this play, it's called Standard Operating
Procedure, cause that's a quote from a doctor in Vietnam who said
that rape in Vietnam was a standard operating procedure. Just about
every soldier did it as his right, as a reward for fighting. And it's a
really horrifying play, it really gets to you and it'll change your life if
you're a sexist person.

Everywhere he turns, John finds the ugliness of sexism. In his own home and on the streets it's the same story:

Like my mother was brought up in a fear mentality. A God-fearing
person, a this-fearing person, a that-fearing person, until she turns
into just a jibbering paranoic. And then the big man comes in and
takes care of her and marries her, the Big John Wayne...and just do
as he says and it'll be alright. You don't have to think, you don't have
to worry anymore, you don't have to cry. No one's going to hit you or
hurt you. And when I think of how she would have been if she hadn't
been interfered with, it's really sad that her life has been half
wrecked...

Same with almost any woman. Like a woman can't walk down the
street without being afraid that someone's gonna go whistle at her and
'Show us ya cunt. Hop into my panel van!' It's really mad.

When John was on the dole, and when he was briefly in paid employment, he kept encountering the victims of patriarchy:

Like you go to someone's house and you say, 'Oh, can I have a drink
of water from your front tap?'

And they say, 'I wouldn't know. My husband isn't...and I'd have
to ask my husband, and...'

Or when I was working on the delivery truck. 'Did my husband ring
you up? Did he say where to put the fridge? I wouldn't know where to
put the fridge...' That sort of thing.

Like Gail in chapter 3 and Claudia in chapter 6, John is also aware of how men are oppressed by sexism, particularly by the dominant style of chauvinistic masculinity which they are pressured to emulate:

I think it'd be a relief to most males to find out that they're not John Waynes... I reckon there'd be a lot of suicides every year because of that...

You've got to have a big swagger. Be big and blunt and everything. 'She's a beauty. It's right.' Or 'They're fucking commos and pooftas'. It's a black-and-white sorta mentality.

Like you mention the word 'sensitive', you can't have any sensitivity involved in someone like that and it must be really hard trying to live a life like that...

Obviously much of John's thinking has evolved over time. Nevertheless his theatre experiences have been highly significant, particularly in crystallising his former feelings and giving them a sharper focus. This is important in terms of the whole thrust of this book. All of the chapters have stressed that people's ideas arise from, and only make sense in, the social and historical context in which they live. The physical conditions under which they live, whether poverty or affluence, exert pressures and constraints over what it is possible or likely that people will think. The same is true for their emotional networks. It makes a lot of difference whether they are part of a supportive friendship network or whether they are isolated and lonely. Chapters 2, 3 and 6 showed this very clearly.

However, people's ideas do not automatically arise straight out of these physical and emotional conditions. They have to pass through an already existing culture which is impregnated with various views of the world. As chapters 4 and 5 made clear, the male view of the world is massively built into contemporary culture. The problem this presents for young women trying to come to terms with their own way of experiencing the world is eloquently captured in Shulamith Firestone's words:

...women have no means of coming to an understanding of what their experience is, or even that it is different from male experience. The tool for representing, for objectifying one's experience in order to deal with it, culture, is so saturated with male bias that women almost never have a chance to see themselves culturally through their own eyes. So that finally, signals from their direct experience that conflict with the prevailing (male) culture are denied and repressed.[22]

When Marg, in chapter 5, talked about rape she voiced the male view of the world. Rapists were sick people and women could 'lead men on'. Yet this male language flew in the face of her own experience of her boyfriend's violence towards her. The last part of that conversation with Marg saw her in the process of repressing this conflict.

Fortunately, repression does not always work, and one of the distinctive features of chapter 6 was the way Claudia broke through the boundaries of male vision and understood how her earlier unhappiness had been due to aspirations tied to a sexist notion of romantic success. With her feminist perspective Claudia could see through the strategies of the chauvinistic males as they attempted to intimidate herself and her friends into returning to the fold.

Maria, who spoke briefly in chapters 3 and 4, broke through this male vision with great suddenness, with an insight that ruptured the abscess of patriarchy and allowed her to understand her experiences through her own eyes. Feminists know this to be a common occurrence and call it the 'click phenomenon':[23]

> *Maria*: It just came, all of a sudden I understood. It was a really necessary thing to happen because so many things I couldn't understand because they'd always been presented in a sexist way or a male point of view, and once I started to have some faith in women and what they were saying, I started to see things from a different angle and find that I could understand things if they were interpreted differently, that I'd always been looking for that, just anything, just even reading.
>
> Dad and I'd go to a film and I never had faith in what I saw or what I understood because it wasn't how he saw it or how the very conditioned women around me saw it.
>
> And I found that I could really understand now, that I could interpret things because I could see it from MY point of view.

The value of youth theatre is that it promotes these kinds of conversions. This can happen because theatre workshops artificially create situations which people would normally only encounter in random and uncontrolled ways. The possibility for redefining experiences is far greater when people can control and shape the way those experiences unfold. They can, moreover, grapple with those experiences with different languages. They can bypass the dominant views of the world, the languages of capitalism, patriarchy, racism and militarism, and forge a view of the world which is authentic to their own experiences.

It is sometimes naively assumed that these repressive languages can be combated on the purely intellectual level. I hope this book has shown how that strategy has only limited use. Most of the attitudes which people expressed through these pages were tightly bound into various psychological strategies. Sometimes these strategies were emotional investments in a decision to stay at school or in a future life as a married mother. At other times they were strategies of survival, attempts to keep battered egos intact. Whatever the case, it is rare to find people's ideas lined up neatly in a row, ready to be knocked over and replaced by another set. People are not often free to simply change their minds through rational persuasion. The emotional loading which some ideas carry keeps them firmly embedded in a person's outlook.

In every chapter it has been apparent that the ideology of individualism obscures the social and historical context in which people and events belong. By ignoring the structures in which individuals operate, individualism leaves the economic arrangements, the social institutions and the power relations unquestioned and enables 'blame the victim' mentalities to flourish. As the earlier chapters made clear, individualism turns attention away from the political ways in which schools are organised because the emphasis is invariably on the 'attitudes' of the students. Similarly, individualism means that fundamental questions about the nature of work in a capitalist society and the failure of the profit motive to generate worthwhile employment opportunities are both ignored in favour of a focus on the characteristics of the unemployed.

Sexist ideology finds a valuable ally in individualism. Again fundamental questions about the nature of social institutions, such as marriage and the family, are ignored when the emphasis is on individuals and their 'failure' to make things 'work'. The power arrangements which underlie sexual relations are also totally obscured while the focus is on the characteristics of individuals, of some people who are 'genuine' and some who are mercenary, of the 'good' blokes and the 'bad'.

In a hierarchical society, the focus on individuals is a classic device for justifying the basically unjust distribution of rewards and access to power experienced by the majority of people who inhabit the lower ranks of the pyramid. According to the ideology of individualism, it is their 'failure'—either their lack of talent, initiative, perseverance or whatever—which is responsible for their being on the bottom of the heap. Within this perspective the simple fact that in a pyramidal hierarchy the great majority will always be on the bottom—irrespective of their characteristics—remains an embarrassing mystery.

Adopting a structural perspective breaks through the mystifications generated by individualism. In all the chapters above, placing individuals inside their larger social and historical context consistently adds a further dimension of understanding to that offered by their own reflections.

It is sometimes objected that this structural approach reduces people to simply the puppets of massive unseen forces and robs them of any 'freewill'. The reply to this is simple: people do make history, but not under conditions of their own choosing. As all the chapters in this book show, young people constantly make decisions and assert control over their lives, *but* not all of them do this equally. The middle-class youths respond to unemployment far differently from their working-class peers, and a large part of this difference is due to the different degree of control they have over what is happening to them. And the reason for these differences? The social arrangements which empower some people and not others. Similarly, the feminist women respond differently to male chauvinism from those trapped within sexist ideology. Again it is a question of the former having access to resources which empower them in their struggles.

'Power' is a double-sided word. It means not only *power over* but also *power to*. Being 'empowered' does not mean exercising power over others but rather gaining power to realise one's fullest potentialities. A necessary condition for such development is control over one's own life, particularly one's physical and cultural environment.

Individuals are always inside structures. It is naive to believe that people can live in some kind of spontaneous or 'natural' mode. The important issue is deciding which structures are empowering and which are oppressive and evolving a political practice which addresses this level of social change.

Notes

1 Official statistics show that 29 per cent of 15- to 19-year-olds are unemployed and looking for full-time work whereas for people over twenty, the figure is 8.5 per cent. *The Labour Force, Australia, Jan., 1983*, (Preliminary) Cat. No. 6202.0, Canberra, ABS, 10 February 1983. The teenage labour market has been particularly vulnerable to two important trends, themselves symptomatic of capitalist restructuring in Australia: a significant contraction in full-time jobs and a steady expansion of part-time job opportunities. See B. Wilson and J. Wyn 'School and Work: What Do Students Think?' in National Clearinghouse on Transition from School *Newsletter* 2, 1, 1983, Dept of Sociology, Research School of Social Science, ANU. See also: Gay Hawkins 'The Teenage Labour Force in Times of Crisis' in *Radical Education Dossier* 10, Summer 1979

2 'A report on *Youth Needs and Public Policies* (Wright and Headlam 1976) makes it clear that the factors associated with work include challenge, variety, autonomy and use of one's abilities. Furthermore, their evidence clearly discounts the myth of the 'workshy' teenager, and emphasises the destructive impact of unemployment: it is 'leisure' that is boring (Wilson and Wyn 1982). Work, therefore, for them is most important for its intrinsic satisfaction, as a source of income, and a measure of personal independence.' Les Cameron, Kerry O'Neill and Bruce Wilson 'Class and Curriculum—a basis for action' in *Radical Education Dossier* 20, Winter, 1983

3 See C. Blakers 'Teenagers: From School to Work—A Summary of the Research: Part 3, School Stayers and School Leavers' in National Clearinghouse on Transition from School *Newsletter* 2, 1, 1983, Dept of Sociology, RSSS, ANU and also J. Wyn and B. Wilson, Class, Gender and Livelihood: some implications for action, paper presented to Sociology Association of Australia and New Zealand conference, Melbourne, August, 1983

4 See ch. 8, 'Media and the Dole Bludger Myth' in Keith Windshuttle *Unemployment, A social and political analysis of the economic crisis in Australia* Penguin Australia, 1979

5 See E. Bakke *The Unemployed Man—A Social Study* London:

Nisbet, 1933 and A Report Made to the Pilgrim Trust *Men Without Work* Cambridge: Cambridge University Press, 1938
6. M. Johoda *Marienthal; the sociography of an unemployed community* Chicago: Aldine-Atherton, 1971
7. CYSS, Community Youth Support Schemes, are local activities centres organised for young unemployed people under 25
8. The Commonwealth Employment Service (CES) is a Commonwealth agency which registers people looking for work and vacancies from employers. To be eligible for unemployment benefits, people must first register with the CES before going on to the Department of Social Security
9. Windshuttle *Unemployment* p. 275
10. Quoted in D. Marsden *Workless: some unemployed men and their families* Penguin England, 1975, p. 197
11. See Jurgen Habermas *Theory and Practice* Boston: Beacon Press, 1973
12. Quoted in E. Wilkinson *The Town That Was Murdered* London: Victor Gollancz, 1939, p. 203
13. See M. Smith and D. Crossley (eds) *The Way Out* Melbourne: Landsdowne, 1975
14. Dale Spender *Invisible Women—The Schooling Scandal* London: Writers and Readers, 1982
15. This discrepancy between aspirations and actual decisions is a common occurence for young women. See E.M. Wakefield, Girls, Science and Technology, paper presented at Conasta XXXII, Adelaide, 16–20 May, 1983. See also S.N. Sampson *Initiatives to Change Girls' Perceptions of Career Opportunities—An Evaluation* Canberra: Dept of Education and Youth Affairs, 1983
16. Spender *Invisible Women* p. 81
17. The Department of Social Security is the Commonwealth department responsible for payment of welfare benefits, including Unemployment Benefits
18. Special Benefits is a short-term general benefit intended to cover situations not covered by other benefits, for example, people under sixteen who are unemployed are not eligible for Unemployment Benefits
19. For example Willis, Corrigan and McRobbie. See recommended reading for publication details
20. For example, the 'ear'oles' in Willis's book
21. HSC: the Higher School Certificate is the matriculation certificate awarded at the end of the final year of High School and is based on public examinations
22. Firestone *The Dialectic of Sex*
23. Phrase quoted in Spender *Invisible Women*

Further reading

PART I: UNEMPLOYMENT

Keith Windshuttle *Unemployment* Penguin, 1979. [An excellent analysis of the current crisis]

Michele Turner *Stuck! Unemployed people talk to Michele Turner* Penguin, 1983 [Interviews with unemployed people about their life without work]

D. Marsden *Workless: some unemployed men and their families* Penguin, 1975. [Interviews with unemployed people in England in the early 1970s]

Peter Hollingworth *Australians in Poverty* Nelson, 1979. [An account of how people are affected by poor housing, low incomes and unemployment]

Wendy Lowenstein *Weevils in the Flour, An Oral Record of the 1930s Depression in Australia* Melbourne, 1978.

George Orwell *The Road to Wigan Pier* Penguin, [An account of unemployment in a coalmining township in the 1930s]

W. Greenwood *Love on the Dole* London, 1965. [A novel about young unemployed people set in the English midlands in the 1930s]

PART II: THE PEER GROUP AND THE FAMILY

Michele Barret *Women's Oppression Today* London: Verso, 1980. [A recent socialist feminist analysis of women's oppression]

Shulamith Firestone *The Dialectic of Sex* Frogmore: Paladin, 1972. [A classic radical feminist analysis from the early 1970s]

Dale Spender *Invisible Women* London: Writers and Readers, 1982. [An analysis of women's education which highlights how classroom interactions consistently discriminate against women]

Ann Oakley *House Wife* Penguin, 1976. [Includes an historical account of domestic labour, an analysis of the sexist myths which perpetuate women's domestic subjugation, and a sociological case study of four housewives]

Joan Barfoot *Gaining Ground* London: Women's Press, 1980. [A novel which perceptively probes the nature of the nuclear family as an institution and its effects on women's autonomy]

Michel Foucault *A History of Sexuality*, Penguin, 1981. [An analysis of sexuality which shows how knowledge, power and sexuality are interrelated]

PART III: CLASS AND SCHOOLING

Bob Connell, Dean Ashenden, Sandra Kessler and Gary Dowsett *Making the Difference, Schools, Families and Social Division* Sydney: George Allen and Unwin, 1982. [A recent study of class and gender socialisation in Australian secondary schools]

Paul Willis *Learning to Labour, How Working Class Lads Get Working Class Jobs* Gower, 1979. [An English study of working-class resistance to the official ideology of schooling]

Paul Corrigan *Schooling the Smash Street Kids* London: Macmillan, 1979. [Similar to Willis but more readable]

Stuart Hall and Tony Jefferson (eds) *Resistance Through Rituals: Youth Subculture in post-war Britain* London: Hutchinson, 1976. [Article by McRobbie and Garber analyses working class women's experiences of schooling]

David Robins and Philip Cohen *Knuckle Sandwich, Growing Up in the Working-class City* Penguin, 1978. [A study of an attempt to set up a youth disco which highlights the boredom and violence of living in an English working-class council estate]

Richard Sennet and Jonathon Cobb *The Hidden Injuries of Class* Vintage Books, 1973. [An American study of working-class attitudes, highlighting their awareness of how their class position has denied them the full development of their capacities]

Index

ageism, 80, 94, 119
America, 24, 149
Andrew, 145
Andy, 28–37, 45, 132
Angela, 70–2
apprenticeships, 124–7, 134
army, 126, 130
assessment, 1–2, 145
attitudes, 9, 11–4, 17–9, 29
authority, 118, 130
autonomy, 53, 72–3, 90, 107, 116

Barbara, 24
Barfoot, Joan, 90
Bill 28–41, 43, 46, 132, 147
'blame the victim', 10, 115
Bob, 28–41
bosses, 36–7, 97, 132–4
bourgeois political theory, 25
bureaucracy, 40, 103

cadets, 128–131, 134, 145–6
capitalism, 16, 24, 46, 134, 152
Carl, 22–3
Carol, 13, 15
CES (Commonwealth Employment Service), 32, 103, 139
Charles, 44–6, 116
Claudia, 43–4, 46, 91–4, 102–8, 149–50, 152
Col, 21–3
commonsense, 25
communism, 40
computers, 3, 76, 115, 133
conceptual tools, 93, 99, 115–116, 152
conformists, 134
correspondence courses, 4

counter culture, 24, 46, 48, 50; Nimbin, 24
courts, 23
curriculum, 29, 116–7, 124, 127–8, 145; 'hidden curriculum', 116–7
CYSS (Community Youth Support Scheme), 30, 34

David, 145
Debbie, 38, 66, 72, 91–103, 107
Department of Social Security, 96–7
discipline, 30, 127–130, 134
divorce, 81, 122, 140–1
dole, 4, 9, 12, 16–17, 41, 113–4, 125–6, 138; dole bludger myth, 15–16, 18–9, 30, 80, 111–5; dole living, 4, 9, 30–2, 34, 37, 45, 49, 50–2, 98, 147–9
Don, 18–20, 128
Donna, 111–23, 124, 136
double standard, 66, 69, 71
drinking, 40, 62, 82, 89, 121–2
drugs, 32–3, 63, 98, 101, 119–21

Eleanor, 76
England, 35
environmentalism, 45

family life, 79–90, 140–1, 144–5
feminism, 11, 46, 104–8, 152, 154
Firestone, Shulamith, 151
Fraser, Malcolm 21, 24, 41, 126, 148
'freedom', 144
friends, 4, 46, 49, 106–7, 119, 137–8
future, 32–3, 81–2, 127–8, 134

Gail, 43, 46–55, 116, 148, 150

Gaining Ground, 90
gender harassment, 74−5, 83
'going out', 60−5, 70, 80, 83, 112
grading, 2−3, 75, 145
Great Depression, 27−8
Greeks, 21, 69−72

Habermas, Jurgen, 40
Hayden, Bill 24, 41
health, 132−3
Hewett, Dorothy, 27
'hidden curriculum' 116−7
hierarchies, 54, 117, 119, 130−5, 153
HSC (Higher School Certificate), 136
'human nature', 24−5
hunger marches, 42

income redistribution, 39, 47−8, 99, 143−4
individualism, 5, 11, 16, 22−5, 39, 40−1, 54, 77−8, 86, 90, 94, 96, 116−7, 122, 128, 131−2, 134, 143, 144−6, 153
industrial democracy, 47−8
inflation, 20, 128
Italians, 21, 68

Janet, 59, 61, 72−75, 79−82, 90, 122
Jason, 69, 72
jobs, 15, 53−5, 97, 125, 131−3, 137, 139; alienating jobs, 10, 44−5, 47, 50, 148; jobs and adult status, 15; job market 12−14, 17, 50, 97, 102. 125−6, 138−9; job search, 9, 12, 14−15, 21−2, 33, 51, 113, 147
John, 147−151

Karen, 1−4

Laura 1−4
learning problems, 29
leisure, 37, 45
Lewis, 124−134
long term unemployed 27−42
Lucy, 17−18, 59−60, 72−5, 77−9, 82

Marg, 20−2, 82−90, 125, 151−2
Maria, 43−6, 67−8, 152
marriage, 20, 81−2, 86−90, 122, 140−4

masculinity, 47, 68, 107, 150−1
Matthew, 15
media, 16, 40−1, 67, 73
Michael, 12, 15
middle class respectability, 50, 52
middle class youth, 43−58, 91−4, 102−8
militarism, 130, 134, 145−6, 152

naturalising 11, 25, 88−90, 112, 134, 139, 142
Nia, 70−2
Nick, 13, 15, 111

Nigel, 14−5
Nimbin, 24

ostracism, 35
outdoor recreation, 45

Pam, 12, 15
parents, 1−2, 22, 30, 43, 49, 63, 72, 80−2, 98, 100, 102, 113−4, 120, 127, 140−1
patriarchy, 24, 46, 69, 72, 80, 86, 88−90, 93−4, 122, 150, 152
Paul, 16, 17
peace rallies, 45
peer group, 17, 59−78, 119−20, 137
political activity, 39−40, 41−2, 98, 149
poverty, 30−1, 39, 41, 59, 148
power relations, 65, 97, 94, 154
pressures, 2, 119−21
private schooling, 136, 146−56
Public Service, 49

racism, 91, 94, 143, 152
rape, 59, 62, 76, 85−6, 91−2, 150−1
religion, 84, 104−5
research (1930s), 27−8
research method, 1, 5
reserve army of unemployed, 36−7
resistance, 30, 117−8, 124, 131
revolutionary actions, 51−2
Richard, 136−145
running away, 59, 121
Ruth, 67, 78, 100−1

Sandy, 9−11, 88
schooling, 1−3, 9−26, 74−6, 95, 99,

106–7, 111–123, 124–35, 136–46; alternative schooling, 24, 43, 45–6, 53, 116, 147; curriculum, 29, 116–7, 124, 127–8, 145; 'hidden curriculum', 116–7; private schooling 136, 146–56; and unemployment, 9, 11–12, 14, 18, 22, 29, 112, 116, 125
'self' and 'other', 13–4, 61–3, 128, 149–50
self-esteem, 2, 22, 26–7, 35, 41, 45, 47, 100, 147
sex, 64–72, 83–4, 119, 121
sexism, 38, 46–7, 66, 80, 105–8, 150–3
sexist ideology, 66–73, 76, 107, 118, 145
'slut', 67, 69
Social Security, Department of, 96–7
Spender, Dale, 74–6
stealing, 18, 31, 39, 148
Stuart, 59, 69, 78, 91, 101–2
Steve, 124–134
strategies, 6, 23, 25, 64–5, 73, 76, 131, 153
strikes, 36, 41, 131
structural perspective, 6, 10–11, 26, 54, 77, 90, 103, 131, 154
Sue, 1–2
suicide, 30, 79, 151
survival, 38, 148

teachers, 2–3, 74–5, 117
technical college, 4

transitory unemployed, 43–58
Trish, 111–23, 124, 136
trust, 120–1

unemployment, 9–58, 91–111, 138, 147–9; and schooling, 9, 11–12, 12, 18, 22, 29, 112, 116, 125; dole, 4, 9, 12, 16–17, 41, 113–4, 125–6, 138; dole living, 4, 9, 30–2, 34, 37, 45, 49, 50–2, 98, 147–9; dole bludger myth, 15–16, 18–9, 30, 43, 80, 111–5; long term, 27–42; reserve army, 36–7; transitory, 43–58; women, 38, 43–58, 91–110
unions, 36, 132
universalising, 12, 17
university, 50, 54–5, 76, 117

virginity, 70–2, 120–1

wealth, 136–45
Windshuttle, Keith, 15, 35
women and careers, 74–5
women's refuge, 50
women and unemployment 38, 43–58, 91–110
work, nature of, 16, 35, 153
work ethic, 19
workers, 36–7, 48, 54, 131–2
working class youth, 27–42, 91–103, 111–135

youth refuge, 20–3, 59, 79, 81, 96, 102
youth theatre, 10, 104, 149–52